As Long As You're In The Car, You're Not Lost!

By Edna Blake

Patsy!
Stay in the car.
and on the road.

Edna Blake

Ecl. 11:4

First Printing, June 2001

For information contact Edna Blake at:
14 Merribrook Court • O'Fallon, MO • 63366
E-mail address: WildSocks@AOL.com
636-978-6320

ISBN: 0-9668906-1-2

Scripture Quotations, used by permission are from:
*The Touchpoint Bible - The New Living Translation 1996,
unless otherwise noted.*

Cover and illustrations by Kathy Allen, St. Peters, MO

Printed in the United States of America.

This book is dedicated to:
My Mom, **Edith Boatwright**, who inspires all of us
to stay in the car unless you have
important business to do for God.
She doesn't drive, but she likes to take little trips
over the river and through the woods.

Table of Contents

Introduction

I have been thinking a lot about the path...the road...and the many detours and changes we face as we travel this road. I am challenged by my thoughts especially when I think about why I am on the road, and the possibilities of where I am going. I finally concluded, I am not always certain about the path but when I am in the car I have hope, and I am confident I will arrive at my destination. I am trusting in the roadmap and my faith in Christ to bring me to my final destination.

This book is about some of the issues I see around me as I am traveling in the car looking out my window. I wanted a safe place to put down my thoughts and the discipline of doing something with what I have been learning.

I am really writing about my process once again. I do not want to be distracted in my journey or lose sight of the path. I am putting the bread crumbs down along the way. Perhaps some of the bread crumbs will resonate with some of the issues you have discovered and God will encourage us both. If the lessons learned have any purpose or value I don't want to misplace them, plus, the issues surrounding us do need to be noted and observed, how else will we find our way home again?

I have been along some challenging paths, our paths come together as we share the journey. I am learning about my incredible God as he walks with me along the path. The Holy Spirit being my constant companion and guide. I am sure you will identify with some of the sights and scenes along the way...and some of the issues viewed from the window as well. I certainly have no final solutions or answers...just some observations from my journey.

Our lives are the journey. The missing portions of the journey are filled in and we understand clearly where we have been but not necessarily where we are going. I included the side trips, the picnics along the shore, the scenic routes when we were lost somewhere in Iowa....all of our experiences have value. I will share some of the word pictures from my journey from my perspective of who I am in Christ.

It is important for me to continue getting out of the driveway, continuing to challenge myself to never stop learning and never stop applying the word of God to my heart and life.

The title of this book comes from a phrase my Mom and I shared a few years back. We lived here years ago in the Greater St. Louis vicinity and moved back from Minnesota. We found ourselves in a whole new world. We also found ourselves lost a great deal of the time. The changes and the population explosion in our little county caused a phenomenal growth spurt. New roads, new buildings and new ways of getting lost.

Mom, being close to ninety, has observed many changes. I was the driver, but she had the experience. We found ourselves getting lost ever so often. Mom's favorite response to my unacknowledged admission of being lost was, "Why don't you stop and ask someone for directions?" I would just continue on...and then she would say, "I think I've seen this before." I would continue driving, but now going a little faster because I realized...we **were indeed lost** and going to be late! The final statement would be, Mom quietly saying, "I think we must be lost." Imagine that!

I turned to her on this particular day, as we had pulled up to a stop light, and said in a very caustic voice, "Mom, do you know that you are in this car?" In her best and most meek of tones, "Yes....I know that." I responded in my higher pitched tone, "Well as long as you're in this car, you're not lost." We started to laugh...and then we laughed some more, I had to pull over to the side of the road...we laughed at ourselves and it broke the tension. As time passed, and we would once again find ourselves **lost**...Mom would say to herself in a very direct but low voice, "I'm in the car and I am not lost." We have taken this humorous event in our lives and tried to apply it to everyday living and life itself, We are *on the Road in the car in the midst of our journey and we are not lost!*

Proverbs 15:24

The path of the wise leads to life above; they leave the grave behind.

Isaiah 48:17-18

The LORD, your Redeemer, the Holy One of Israel, says: I am the LORD your God, who teaches you what is good and leads you along the paths you should follow.

Chapter One

WE'RE ON THE ROAD...

WITH HEALTHY FAMILIES IN THE CAR!

"How in the world did we miss that turn? I don't think the sign was marked clearly enough, or I didn't have enough time to respond to the sign, and I completely missed the turn. Why don't they make signs a little more driver friendly?"

Traveling with the Family!

We used to love to pile into our old station wagon...known today as the Van...the SUV...or the RV...and down the road we would go. Traveling with the family is a life changing experience. It can make or break a family. It is supposed to be part of *the family bonding times, but family bonding times are not always so bonding!*

Family bonding times are not always pleasant, in fact, some of those times are stressful and draining. Being a family in a car or station wagon or in a house, or in an apartment...takes thought and determination and certainly, the Grace of God. Families...Healthy Families just don't happen!

Healthy Families Take Time and Care! → → → → → →

Any trip takes time and planning. You can't just walk out to the car and say, let's go! We are on our way...we are out of here...Moving out! It takes a lot of preparation...the laundry preparation alone...then getting the suitcases packed, planning for 10 days...the little suitcases distributed among the family members! What a challenge? You remember! Plus, some families take the family pets along. It's down right scary.

The trip, and the family take time and care. The family is very important to God. God established the family and God blesses the family. The family is one of God's Evangelistic Tools for winning people to Christ. The Holy Spirit uses families to introduce others to Jesus. God wants to use the family in the Twenty First Century to reach the lost. The family is one place where we see God at work. He starts with us in our Family Unit in our car, or Station Wagon, RV, Van, or SUV.

God relates to us and our family and he calls us to relate to those around us. We bring others into the family of God by being a healthy family in a lost world. We are in our cars on the highway of life traveling down the road, traveling at different speeds...we are all on the road. We are salt and we are light. We bring our family dynamics into the lives of others...in the little league, in the school system, in the work place, and most assuredly, to our neighborhoods. We are the Church and part of the Family of God.

God is the God of the multitude and the God of the individual... and the family. He is the God of the highways in our lives and also the God of the byways. He is the God of the big things that concern us and the little things. He does mighty works and sees to the smallest detail. Nothing we face is too big for Him to handle, and He will not overlook our tiniest need.

The concept of how important the family really is helps us to better understand why the family today is under attack. The enemy will do whatever it takes to disrupt the peace of the family. Divorce, abuse, materialism, un-forgiveness and an indifference to God all are taking us down some dead end paths. When a Mom and Dad are in place in the family it is a powerful tool, bringing others to Christ. When husbands and wives and kids are on the road traveling together in full view of the world it makes an impression. It gives hope to those who are struggling and looking for help with their family trip. Anytime, you can get the whole family together for anything...it makes an impression.

> *Our little family would travel down the road, Bill and I would be sitting up in front...just smiling as we passed others by...our boys would be in the back seat making faces and I won't tell you all they might have been doing...because I didn't know it at the time...and God gives grace to mothers who don't always know what the family may be doing.*

Do you believe in your family? We know that God does and he wants healthy families to be established throughout the world. **Admitting that we are lost and having a problem is the beginning of a great trip and can bring healing and hope to the marriages and families that are on a collision course. STOP, LOOK, AND LISTEN!**

It would be interesting to calculate how many hours over the years we have spent lost and going in the wrong direction. **What finally caused you to admit you were lost?** It is usually a crisis, a need to find the rest area, a need to find fuel, a normal need. A crisis moves us to stop and ask for directions. A crisis in the family can be the opportunity God uses to get our attention and to help us get back on the main road headed in the right direction. Sometimes, because of a crisis we are forced to get out of the car, regroup and get back on the road.

We all have those times when relating to one another is almost like we're carving words out of stone and no sounds are being heard. The enemy is trying to get us off of the main road and on to some side street. Lost! True, we can take the scenic route instead of the main highway, but it is by design, it is our plan. No one chooses to be lost without a plan. We are anxious to be in control and to not appear foolish...we are concerned about the path for our families.

> *I would go anywhere with my grandson Josh...he has a way of knowing where he has been and how to get there again. It is truly amazing! He could tell you every turn and every road from his house in St. Louis, to our house in Duluth, even as a small child. If I should need to take a trip today, I would want him to come along as the navigator. He is that good! Wisdom is connecting with someone who has been down the road before and allowing them to guide you to the place you need to be.*

When the family is in trouble...seek wise counsel. *Look for the Map or find a navigator!*

Psalm 90:12

Teach us to make the most of our time, so that we may grow in wisdom.

1. Pray and seek to love each other unconditionally.
2. Forgive and Forgive...and then give... and start over again.
3. Establish healthy communication with each other and if that means getting a counselor to come along side of you both then do it.
4. Don't expect old behaviors to change over night...but believe they can change.
5. Don't revisit every past grievance. Shame and blame will not help.
6. Seek for yourself to be closer to God and determine how to follow him better.

7. Participate in worship, and fellowship with other believers.

It all sounds so simple...seven little steps. We want solutions, a quick fix. We want to always take the shortest route. We want the trip to have no bumps and no detours. Just give me the map! I know I can do it...but we forget the healing factor of the Holy Spirit. We forget the Balm of Gilead. We forget that God really cares about our families. We can be lost for the purpose of God revealing more of Himself to us. Families are under attack, and the road can be really confusing especially when the members of the family are going in so many directions...but do not lose heart!

Proverbs 12:26

The godly give good advice to their friends; the wicked lead them astray.

The family starts with the parents and their parents. If the family is to travel any length of time along the road of life it has to have stability and it has to have direction. The family is made up of individuals but in the beginning the parents are responsible for planning the trip and giving time to the preparation, showing concern for each of the passengers. The map, the word of God is so important for maturing the whole family. The word must be honored in the household by the parents and by its members. We learn about God's directions from being men and women, boys and girls, practicing the wisdom of the word. We grow as we experience practicing our faith as we live out our journey.

Proverbs 14:2

Those who follow the right path fear the LORD, those who take the wrong path despise him.

Inside of the car we find so many distractions. We are on the move going down the road. We are people who are stressed to the max, running to and fro...we need to look at what we have going on in our family car. Our family unit needs to plan times of rest. We cannot drive forever! We need rest stops.

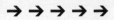
1. In our busyness, we do not know how to take time out and just relax and enjoy each other without a planned agenda or meeting the goals of all the family members. The Rest Area is for a purpose.

2. We have forgotten what it is like to have quietness and peace in the car. We are not in our homes, we are in our cars with the mobile phone, the radio, the C.D. player, the computer, games in the back seat, and sometimes even a television complete with videos and games, along with other noise related activities going a mile a minute!

3. We are unable to be satisfied. We are always needing more and more stimulation for the children. We have to have a bigger TV, a bigger pool, a larger family room, bigger and better birthday parties. More, more and more! Not to mention a bigger car!

4. We have forgotten rules and structure are good for families. We need healthy guidelines. The road signs are helpful in giving us needed directions and encouragement. Only 10 more miles can be hopeful information when looking for the rest room.

5. We have become doers of the word...and by that statement, I mean running to serve and do at the local Church without taking time to do the maintenance for our families first. We had better do a maintenance check on the car at the appropriate time or the red light will go on and we know what that means! HELP! The same is true for our families.

6. Worries and concerns need to be put out on the table and addressed. This is not happening in many homes and families. The dad is concerned about one thing and the mom has another issue. The dad may be concerned about the financial status of his family and his business opportunities. The mom may be concerned about the children, about how they look, their social life, their education, their world. It is an accident waiting to happen unless parents get on the same

16

road. We have to give it up and over to the Lord. We are equipped to solve problems in our homes and cars. It helps to involve the family in planning the journey and problem solving.

7. We often compare our families with other families. We set our standards by other families rather than seeking what God has called us to be and do. We work to achieve what others have. We may need a larger van...but don't allow the need to have a bigger van be because our neighbor has a bigger one...let it be because we need a bigger van to get us all out on the road again.

The family, the Healthy Family is so important to God. I am going to deal with single parents and blended families...a family can be healthy even in blended family situations. God does hate divorce but it is not the unpardonable sin and we know that people do recover from divorce but it is painful and it does leave a scar upon the family members. I work with divorced people all the time and I see their pain and anger. They did not plan for their families to be disrupted. It happens, and they have to continue on, but their advice is to work in your present family asking God to help you as you pursue health!

God wants us to rely upon Him rather than our service, he wants our worship and our adoration before he wants to hear our journey plans. He wants us to learn to plan our journey with Him. He wants us to know when to stop at the rest stop. He wants us to figure out when enough is enough. He wants us to get out of the car and walk around and enjoy the beauty of our world while we are experiencing our journey. He does desire for all of us to have Healthy Families.

Healthy Families Deal with Their Feelings!

Do not be ruled by your feelings. When I try to ignore my feelings I am no longer in control of them, they are in control of me. When I think of me controlling my feelings, I must admit I cannot do anything without the Spirit of God in my life. I may be talking about self-control, but it has to start with Holy

Spirit control. Start identifying what is truth and what is a lie. We must come to a point where we can understand the difference between our attitude and our feelings. We can often set the tone by changing our attitude about how we are feeling.

Bill and I wrote long ago in a book, things that were helpful to us in dealing with our marriage. We had been married for many years but we never stopped being a family and we never stopped working on our relationship. We were working on a Workshop dealing with, Healing in Broken Relationships.

He wrote about me...The special quality in you I like best is the same quality which initially attracted me to you 32 years ago...your lively, spunky warm outgoing personality. When I think of that quality in you I feel warmed and accepted, desired and excited to be around you.

He wrote about himself...The special quality in me I like best is the quality of quietness and measured reflection which is a part of my process of making decisions and judgments. I feel a sense of confidence and inner quietness when I know I am able to make decisions and judgments in that way.

I know he didn't always see me that way...and I can tell you he did not always feel this way about himself. We were committed to the Lord and therefore, we were committed to giving 100% to our marriage and each other. Our children learned about perseverance by watching us work at our relationship. It was hard work, it was a discipline at times and it took talking about our feelings and our attitudes honestly to get us through some of those difficult times. We would sometimes yell...mostly me, Bill in his quiet way, would just remind me, "Which one of the fruits of the Spirit is that?" I could go down the road for miles without a word...especially if my feelings had been denied and I felt rejection. It's a long trip if the silence is not balanced by communication.

We were very different in many ways but because God had put us together, we were a perfect fit. I needed him...and he needed me...and we both needed to depend upon the Lord for our marriage and our fami-

ly survival. **The journey needed us both. I learned about how to survive in our journey in preparation for my journey as a single woman. I learned so much as a passenger before becoming the driver.**

Couples and families learn about respect in the car. They learn that not everyone can talk, not everyone can sit in the front seat...not everyone can drive. The family outing in the car needs to be a pleasant experience. We must learn to get along with each other, to be respectful of each other, the space, and concerns of others. We need to listen to their ideas about where we need to stop next time for lunch. Respect is a great way of expressing our genuine love for each other.

> *"Mom, he's breathing on me! Mom, he's touching me! Mom, I'm hungry! Mom, I have to go to the bathroom! Mom, I think I am going to be sick! The windshield wipers are making too much noise, could you turn them down? I'm not sure I can hold it any longer."*

Just try enjoying the trip with this going on in the back seat.

Traveling With or Without Children is an Aspect of the Trip!

Life has many curves and detours. I talk and visit with many young couples who have children and those who don't have children. The concerns about parenting can be very different but it is clear, we are not totally prepared for this part of the trip. The path is not always so direct. The road may require some creative driving staying tuned to the demands of the road and the journey. It can feel very much like you are driving in a patch of ground fog. We are hoping for the fog to lift so we can pursue the journey with a little more assurance of what we may be facing and a clearer sense of direction. We feel good when we can at least recognize some familiar sights so we can get our bearings. When we are out there and the path is not clear, we are looking for directions, signs, and sights that will encourage us, and the knowledge that we are indeed, headed in the right direction at last. It takes courage and confidence in the Lord to continue on in this part of the journey. Raising a family is not easy.

Couples without children are still in the car...and they are indeed a family. I think sometimes, it can feel very alone in the car without a family. I sometimes miss the family when I am driving on a long trip alone. I can understand why people take their pets on trips. I am always glad to have Mom in the car with me...she is a good companion and she doesn't bark.

Children are a Blessing From the Lord!

I remember so well the discussion Bill and I had about children before we were married. He wanted five, I didn't have sense enough to know what I wanted. I thought children would be fine, however many I had, children would be fine. I knew I liked children...because I had been one...and I liked childhood. It was a constant adventure and I knew children would be fun. I was an only child and I wanted to surround myself with these little fun people. Can you see where I am going with this? I knew nothing about a very important part of the journey, all I really knew was that I wanted to be on the same road with families who had children in their car. It never even occurred to me that children would not be part of my family. I was so naive.

I am sure couples without children in the car, didn't see it as a major concern early in their journey, but as they traveled along, it did become a focus. I do hear some couples talk about not wanting children and some of them have made that choice for various reasons, but for me, I cannot imagine my life without my sons and grandchildren but choices are determined and life goes on.

Some choices are not our choices, and we find ourselves on a very long lonely road. It is not anything like what we imagined for ourselves and our plan for the journey. It is a hard and difficult time for any couple who desire and want children and find the car is empty! Barrenness was not socially accepted in the times of the Bible and it is hard for some couples today. I know a single woman who has never married, and she expressed this thought, "the saddest part about my life is, I never had any children." She has given to a lot of children and she has found some satisfaction in service for the Lord...but this is her comment.

Psalm 102:28

The children of your people will live in security. Their children's children will thrive in your presence.

The one legacy we have sometimes is our children. We may gather souvenirs from our travels, we may bring back rocks from our adventures in the country...but we had better bring home our children or our trip is just another trip. Children add fun and excitement to our family memories. It is often how the children viewed the trip that gives the journey real meaning and purpose as we view the trip from our easy chairs and remember our years of raising the family. It was a stressful time, but how the children enjoyed the trip was a high priority for most parents. We take along games, we bring special treats, we bring our little presents to give to them along the way...we plan, so their journey will not seem so long and boring. We point out special places of interest and we remember to stop and let them wade the creek on hot days.

I remember the first trip Bill and I took alone...on the motorcycle. It was strange. I kept wanting to call and check in on the children. He reminded me..."they will be fine!" They were teens and I tried to be glad that we had taken off on our adventure...but in the back of my mind I knew they were dealing with the aspect of experiencing what it was like to be left, "Home Alone." I shudder to think about those times now... knowing them as well as I do...I know they did not miss us at all. They had trips to plan and places to go. Growing up is hard on parents and teens.

"Children are an inheritance from the Lord."

We can, of course, pick up hitchhikers...we can adopt and

bring these little people into our families. One of my friends has a little adopted child and she is a joy and blessing to their lives. They have one son who is their biological child and now they have Elizabeth...she has brought to their family many opportunities of learning they would never have known without her presence in their lives.

Linda expresses that she is glad she has a boy and a girl...it has brought her a sense of fulfillment.

They had to travel many miles to adopt her, across a country and an ocean, but she is their special gift from the Lord. I know of others who have cared for children as foster parents and they have found making room in their home or in their car to be a special blessing. It is not for all families. Not everyone wants children and not every family will have children, but if this is part of your dream it can be a very positive thing and adds variation to the journey.

We are on the Road with Healthy Families and it is a significant journey.

The Confusion of Parents!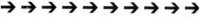

Have you ever spent time driving around confused not exactly knowing where you are and when you even got lost? Being confused as a parent is not something we have to think about, it just happens. I don't recall when I came home from the hospital getting the manual for raising any of our children. I don't believe Dr. Dobson had written any of his books at that point. I am sure the secular world was on top of it and had many ideas about raising children but for us, it was a time of confusion and learning. It was a crash course, and we were just trying to survive any major accident along the way. We might have figured it out for Mike and Tim, but then Dan came along and he didn't fit any of the previous learned routes. In fact, we were challenged to make a whole new road, with Dan...we couldn't just fill in the pot holes.

A New Road...and a New Way of Going Down the Road!

THINKING...that three hours at a movie is harmless for the child, but that two hours of church and Sunday School are too much for his or her nervous system is unhealthy thinking.

GIVING...him or her a quarter for the collection and buying them a CD or a Video game, reveals a parents sense of values, and it will produce a proportionate giver in the future.

LETTING THEM...be on the computer or play their music, or watch their television programs for hours on end and not allowing time to pray with them, read to them from the Bible, talk to them about what is happening in their lives is not acting in their best interest and teaches them about how to be inconsistent in their spiritual walk with the Lord.

BEING...careful to ensure that the children do their homework, get to little league practice, know all the rules of being a scout, but never show any concern if they are learning the word of God is not going to produce healthy godly children. **God is faithful to His Children, and His Word.**

SAYING...to your child, you can make up your own mind about whether or not you should attend church is shirking parental responsibility. We need to lead by example and set the pace that is consistent with the teachings of the Bible for how we bring up our children.

Parents are still responsible to God for what goes on during the journey. We can take them along and we can introduce them to travel, but eventually they will be driving themselves and they need to know where they are going and who they will take with them as part of their journey. We need to set for them good examples and give clear directions for their future as fellow travelers.

When Josh started learning to drive, I rode with him and so did his Granny...it was a little scary. He had the skills and he knew the function of the car much better than I did, but he needed the practice. He did not come to this place in his life of being the driver without having some preparation from his parents. Their counsel and training paid off. The first time he drove out to my house to mow my lawn was such a high time for all of us. I was glad to see him drive up in the driveway. He was coming to mow my lawn and he had driven himself.

I had suffered a heart attack earlier that year and my neighbors had been mowing for me...but to have my grandson come mow my lawn, it was just neat! He could spend some time with me and have a little bite to eat, it was very special. He was a full-fledged driver...on the road with traffic and his life ahead of him. He was no longer just a passenger, he was the driver. The passengers do grow up to be the drivers and we need to remember they know the speed limit too.

Families Sometimes Take Two Cars! ➔ ➔ ➔ ➔ ➔ ➔

We have to remind ourselves that the blended family is a reality. I hope that I have not lost you already along the way because I have had so much to say about the family. We need to note and have an appreciation for the Blended Family...they are sitting in our pews in our churches and they need our support and prayers. It is a very difficult task raising a blended family. It is a task that requires a lot of grace and skills and the Blended Family drives two cars.

Blended Families are happening at an uncharted pace. I don't think the church was prepared for the blended family and how to incorporate them into the body takes skill and prayer. We need to shift gears and recognize men need to be in the

Sunday School class setting...teaching and guiding our young people. Some of the children do not see Godly men modeling healthy behaviors in their everyday lives. We need men to model good things for them from the word, especially, if their Dad is not a Christian. Sometimes, children are being raised by the grandparents and they need to see other Mom's and Dad's leading them with positive examples of a Mom and a Dad.

Children staying in both homes every other weekend is taken for granted by some kids today. Getting dropped off and picked up, exposing them to two different worlds. Vacations being spent with one parent at a time. They are forced to adjust to the rules at one home and then the following week go back to the other home. It is stressful for parents and children. Some highways have several different speeds and the vehicle has to go down the road. Some of us are only traveling a short distance but we have to learn to adjust our speed accordingly. It may require an adjustment on the part of the driver, the passengers are not always aware of the need for controlling the foot pedal. We need to pray and ask for help in giving directions to those with blended families in the car.

The children attending two different churches on a not so regular basis need to be recognized. Making them welcome and accepting them any time they come makes the journey less stressful for them. God knows they are dealing with things some of us have never had to endure or experience.

The children did not get a vote and the adjustment of riding in two cars takes learning some additional skills.

Road Rage...and Anger! → → → → → → → → → → →

The family is a place where anger and rage often occur. When someone pulls out in front of you and the words come out... "The jerk! What do they think they are doing?" It is out there and it is too late to recover the words. Racing in and out of traffic in several lanes of on-going traffic can be hard on the nerves, especially if you are late for an appointment. Trying not to get angry while driving in the real world takes a lot of self-control...or should I say, Spirit control.

I have observed in the little Court where I live, **a modern day parable...**

> *The little children in my Court are busy driving those miniature battery run cars...they put their babies in tiny car seats, they even have passengers. Andrea, Alex, Kaitlyn and Jacob, run up and down the side walks, and out into the Court street. Pretty soon, you might see Cathy and Amber coming out to join them in their miniature automobiles. They occasionally pick up hitch-hikers. I have noticed and observed how they behave while driving. The older sister might say, "sit down or you're getting out! This is the last time I am going to speak to you about that!" "You are not coming shopping with me anymore if you can't behave!" They are perfect at mimicking what they have observed and now practice as little drivers.*

These children come from good homes...and their parents express love while caring for them. The parents are often in the Court playing with them and they are watching out for them guarding them against any destructive play. We need to guard our hearts!

Our anger, our attitudes, our driving manners rub off on the passengers. We must get a grip and we must learn to adjust our attitude while driving and while trying to live within our little family unit. Families can be a hot bed for hostility if not dealt with on a regular basis. Parental abuse is not a topic we want to discuss here but must be faced from time to time. Respect and care have to be a primary concern we express in our family units.

Ephesians 4:2-3

Be humble and gentle. Be patient with each other,

making allowance for each other's faults because of your love. Always keep yourselves united in the Holy Spirit, and bind yourselves together with peace.

Ephesians 4:17-27

With the Lord's authority let me say this: Live no longer as the ungodly do, for they are hopelessly confused. Their closed minds are full of darkness; they are far away from the life of God because they have shut their minds and hardened their hearts against Him. They don't care anymore about right and wrong, and they have given themselves over to immoral ways. Their lives are filled with all kinds of impurity and greed.

But that isn't what you were taught when you learned about Christ. Since you have heard all about Him and have learned the truth that is in Jesus, throw off your old evil nature and your former way of life, which is rotten through and through, full of lust and deception. Instead, there must be a spiritual renewal of your thoughts and attitudes. You must display a new nature because you are a new person, created in God's likeness—righteous, holy, and true.

So put away all falsehood and tell your neighbor the truth because we belong to each other. And don't sin by letting anger gain control over you. Don't let the sun go down while you are still angry, for anger gives a mighty foothold to the Devil."

Ephesians 2:19-21

So now you Gentiles are no longer strangers and foreigners. You are citizens along with all of God's holy people. You are members of God's family. We are His house, built on the foundation of the apostles and the prophets. And the cornerstone is Christ Jesus himself. We who believe are carefully joined together, becoming a holy temple for the Lord.

WORTHY EVENTS TO REMEMBER ALONG THE WAY...

1. What was the most memorable trip you and your family ever took? Why?

2. Do you see yourself as the driver, the back seat driver, a passenger, a hitchhiker picked up along the way...or standing by the road still waiting? Has the role in your family changed for you recently?

3. Describe why it takes so much energy to take a trip? Why do families take so much energy? Do you see any similarities?

4. Do you feel like you have taken off on your own path but have faced some distractions along the way? Perhaps, too busy to spend quality time with your family and you're starting to sense you're losing sight of the goal for your adventure. Remember to Stop, Look, and Listen.

5. Spend some time praying for the families in your circle and acknowledge that God is still on the throne and He has a heart for all families.

6. Maybe you are a single parent, or in a blended family. I encourage you not to give up your goals for your healthy family. It may look a little different, but you can have spiritual health in your family as well. Never lose sight of His plan for your lives.

Jesus was very busy with his life too. Each day was packed with people, demands, and ministry. He traveled from place to place by foot or donkey. He taught and he preached, he healed the sick and he cast out demons but he never panicked.

He expressed anger and got rid of the money changers who were corrupting the place of prayer. He didn't have any fast means of transportation...yet he functioned in peace. He had enough time to do each day the Father's will. Children and families take time and we cannot lose sight of the value of each family.

Chapter Two

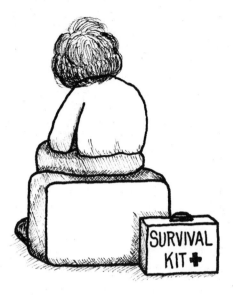

WE'RE ON THE ROAD...

WITH SINGLENESS AND SERENITY!

My journey was interrupted when Bill died!

I was in the car on this nice, little safe journey. It seemed to me that everything was in place...and then the car just stopped. I didn't have a driver. I didn't know where the car insurance papers were kept. I didn't know what was supposed to be in the glove compartment. I knew that extra napkins for wiping the windshield or cleaning up spills was in the glove compartment but I didn't know that important papers about insurance and other important information was supposed to be in the glove compartment. I didn't know about car inspections, emissions inspections, and making sure you kept your paid voucher for taxes together with the other receipts, that kind of thinking was way out there for me. Bill had taken care of it all. I can tell you, I made several trips to the license bureau because I didn't know what to bring. His death was a major disruption to my journey and he was finally at the end of his journey.

I know I just sat in the car for a long time.
I was numb. I was frozen in time.

"As Long As You're in the Car, You're not Lost!"

Suddenly Single! → → → → → → → → → → → →

My journey became very different. The destination seemed really unimportant. I got so caught up in the *now* of my journey and *"what do I do now?" My main concern was for NOW...and my new little world.* I felt so totally alone without a plan or a map. I had no trip guide made up for me, I had never taken this route before.

We never look for the signs that give us new directions for where we are going because we are convinced we will not need to go that way. We have been so desensitized and we certainly do not want to deal with the topic, we ignore any signs or indications from the Lord that our trip could change. My mother was a widow...and I knew other widows, but I never expected to be a widow...even though I had lived with Bill's health problems for three and one half years knowing the time was short. I just could not face the road being swallowed up before me, while I was still trying to go down the road. But that is exactly what happened! Death is so final...even with the hope of seeing him again on the other side.

Isaiah 25:8a (paraphrased)

God will conquer death.

I Corinthians 15:54-58

When this happens—when our perishable earthly bodies have been transformed into heavenly bodies that will never die—then at last the Scriptures will come true:

"Death is swallowed up in victory. O death, where is your victory? O death, where is your sting?"

> *For sin is the sting that results in death, and the law gives sin its power. How we thank God, who gives us victory over sin and death through Jesus Christ our Lord!*

I was totally unprepared for this part of the journey, even though I knew at Christmas Bill had only six months to live unless God saw fit to give us a miracle. He passed away in May, 1993. I had to find a new map and I needed to know how long I would be stalled on the road, so I started looking for my Survival Kit...and I called out to God, on the car phone, "HELP! its me, and I think I am really, really lost! Could you please help me NOW?"

Survival Kit for Emergencies!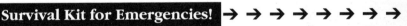

I had no idea what was in the Survival Kit. I was totally unprepared. I am learning about the tools in my survival kit and how they are useful for assisting me along the way. This journey is personal for me but we could be on similar journey, you on yours, and me on mine. God has provisions for both of us.

▽ I discovered that singleness is the gift no one wants.

1 Corinthians 7:7c

God gives some the gift of marriage, and to others he gives the gift of singleness.

I am learning to accept this gift that I discovered in my Survival Kit!

▽ Singleness forces us to change some of our choices.

Where and how we live, now comes into play. We are often forced to get a new vehicle because we no longer need the truck. We no longer need the motorcycle, or the canoe. Singleness may be something you need to think about before it happens.

In the case of divorce, people can feel totally lost and stalled in the car as well. They do not know what to expect. Our lives have been uprooted and we feel partially destroyed. The familiar and safe passages are no longer there. The road upon which

31

we have been traveling has become under construction.

▼ We may need to consider a designated driver...not because we are drunk...but we are not able to drive at this time.

Jesus and the Holy Spirit stepped up in my time of need...and He became my designated driver. I was so glad He was in the kit. I have two designated drivers. My guide the Holy Spirit and my constant friend, Jesus.

It is a very good thing to come along side and help others when the singleness thing hits our lives and our world as we have known it is swallowed up and the road too. We can help others if we have been down the road before. I sold both cars because I had driven Bill to the hospital 17 times in the previous 3 years in those cars and I needed a car to drive that had no history with me and my trips to the hospital.

Singleness is an Emotional Roller Coaster → → → →

The car is speeding at a fast pace, the curve is ahead and you can't find the brakes. It feels like you are going down the hill in a runaway car...you are devastated for awhile but then your life returns, not the old life but a new life...and you find a way to continue in the journey.

I had grief but I did not have guilt, and I did not have regret. It simply meant I had grief without regret about the things I should have done and said to Bill. We had processed so much of our lives together, we were accustomed to talking about tough issues, we spent hours discussing our past, *and my future.* Bill was my very best friend and he really gave me wise counsel. Not everyone finds this tool in their kit...and if we do not possess this component and we do not find it in our Survival Kit, God will provide. He sends help to us from His vast world of resources. He is the God of all Comfort and He will provide.

The Holy Spirit just came along side of me as the Comforter and I grew closer to Him during the difficult time of transition. I was in such pain, but was forced to rely upon Him rather than trying to rely upon myself. The Holy Spirit will be with us throughout our journey. He gives us boldness and confidence to carry on. We can actually get in the drivers seat with calm assurance, knowing that He will be driving for us. It feels like we are on remote control. I did things, went places and didn't remember how I got there or what I said. It is true. I was on remote control and Jesus was driving for me.

Serenity, and Traffic! → → → → → → → → → → →

Do you remember those times when you drove from point A to point B...and you didn't remember how you got there? You didn't see anything, you just drove.

> *My friend Linda, is so good at this, she can do her nails, make-up, take notes, and listen to a tape all at the same time while she is driving...and I am sure, she is on the mobile phone at times while driving through the traffic on to her destination. Recently she shared with me that she has had times of being on two phones at once. She is amazing!*

We need to allow God to take over for us, we are one in Christ and especially in our singleness. We must agree with God that what He says in His word, we will accept and believe about ourselves and about Him. Driving anywhere without knowing He has it under control is serious. I am learning to just rest with the Cruise Control on...God is all knowing! He is in charge of the speed I travel as I continue down the highway.

Sometimes we have to guard against being too serene. We can have a tendency to drop out, or avoid taking any trips at all. These are actions that lead to false security. We need to think and consider the possibility of our new life as being a new adventure with Christ. It is a challenge we face as we develop our ongoing relationship with God while driving on this new divided highway. We can be assured, we will arrive safe, unfrazzled, cool, calm, and collected!

Philippians 1:6

And I am sure that God, who began the good work within you, will continue His work until it is finally finished on that day when Christ Jesus comes back again.

P...Pray

R...Resist the enemy's tactics

A...Acknowledge your pain

I...Ignore anything that would discourage you

S...Savor the moment

E...Enter into His Presence with Thanksgiving

Singleness allows us to know God in a fresh new way. This new relationship with him is like a jump-start which energizes our worn out batteries...we can now proceed with confidence.

We must choose to get out of the driveway and on to the road... and experience this new found peace from the Peace Giver.

John 14:1-7

"Don't be troubled. You trust God, now trust in me. There are many rooms in my Father's home, and I am going to prepare a place for you. If this were not so, I would tell you plainly. When everything is ready, I will come and get you, so that you will always be with me where I am. And you know where I am going and how to get there."

"No, we don't know, Lord," Thomas said, "We haven't any idea where you are going, so how can we know the way?"

Jesus told him, "I am the Way, the Truth, and the Life. No one can come to the Father except through me. If you had known who I am, then you would have known who my Father is. From now on you know him and have seen him."

We cannot go before our Time...and until that time...We need to experience...

Joy in the Journey! → → → → → → → → → → → →

I hate it when someone tells me…"Count it all Joy!" I know this is a helpful statement but when you are trying to apply the truth of this statement to your life…it sounds shallow and hollow and impossible!

James 1:2-4

Dear brothers and sisters, whenever trouble comes your way, let it be an opportunity for joy. For when your faith is tested, your endurance has a chance to grow. So let it grow, for when your endurance is fully developed, you will be strong in character and ready for anything.

You knew this part was coming…patient endurance…it is one of the guideposts along the way, but we stop and look at it and then move on going at our normal pace. I just can't do one more thing, I am not going to do anything more. I need time to find myself…and then it happens! God says, get over yourself and look around you. There is a whole new world…and you are still part of it.

Get Over Yourself Edna! → → → → → → → → → →

Getting over myself was taking on a totally new ministry…

The Singles Ministry in my church needed a new category. I did not want to do some of the activities the younger singles were doing…but I certainly did want to have fun. I went to my pastor and he said, "we do need a group for your age but do you think we have many people in the church interested enough to be involved in this ministry?" A ministry that would involve, "Seasoned Seniors?" I thought it was needed, if for no one else but me.

Along with several others, we invested some time into the lives of Tanner, Leon, Sylvia, Bob, Barb, Maxine, Linda, Betty, Marilyn, Susan, Bonnie, Vicky, Carol, Jeanie, Ruth,…and the list goes on…**ON TRACK** became a reality. The younger group was called, **On Tour**...and we, the **On Track** Group became the mature group, *the Seasoned ones.*

On Track! → → → → → → → → → → → → → → →

This ministry has saved me from self pity and loneliness.

We laugh and study the Bible together. We plan and do retreats and getaways, we travel and take Mystery Trips...those little mystery trips where only the Leadership Team knows where we are going. We rent a van...and take some cars...and down the road we go. It will be some place of interest and a day of fun! You can count on it. We take the day and we visit, we sing, we eat together, pray together and the ministry combination of Service and Togetherness...becomes a sure cure for the blues.

We are on the road again with a new bunch of friends and a new perspective. There is joy in the journey...and we continue to love and support one another in our new roles as singles getting acquainted with the second leg of our journey. Some of our friends have gotten married and what celebrations we have for them. It is a party whenever we get together.

Our first Annual Easter Sunrise Service was a very special time. We had been discussing how the Resurrection made a difference in our lives...in other words, how had Christ given us a new life and brought joy and hope into our lives as a single person? The discussion was great. We had deep sharing. We finished with prayer...and then it happened! It was a cold morning for our area, and it was early in the morning before sunrise...

I had just asked that question, "How has God and the Resurrection of Christ made a difference in your life?"

Bob stood up, took off his shoes and jumped into the little lake surrounding the gazebo where we were having our worship time...in he went...he had on a tie, which for Bob was a rare occasion in of itself...a major belly flop and a huge splash! Ginny grabbed me...I thought for a moment, we were jumping in as well. It was crowd panic! Most of us were in shock...he came up out of the shallow lake...and we were all so glad he hadn't been hurt. I was waiting to see what in the world had provoked this demonstration of total abandonment at this quiet early morning worship time in the park. We listened with amazement and wonder.

As he was drying off and putting a blanket around himself, he told us that earlier in his life, he used to drink to the point of being out of control, and on the weekends especially. The weekends were lost to him. He would hear on Monday mornings what a great guy he was...how much fun he was...and how bold and outgoing he was...but he couldn't remember because he was under the influence of something outside of the Holy Spirit. He could be those things and do those things as the, "life of the party under the influence and control of alcohol," but now he was a Christian. Christ had made a huge difference in his life. Bob wants a real life and real expressions of who he is as a Christian to be a reality.

He wanted to do something that day bold and out-landish...and on Monday he wanted to remember it...the great thing about this story is that we will always remember it as well. What a Hoot! I can tell you, Bob brings lots of joy to us as we watch him grow and change right before our eyes. God is healing his life. His path has many new stages and steps. Walking in the Spirit....brings us joy beyond belief!

We are growing in our faith...we are laughing and making new plans. We have a Care Group that meets on Fridays...we call our time, "Free Fridays." If you are free on Friday, we invite others to come for food, fellowship, friendship, Bible Study, and our own brand of prayers and concerns. It is the highlight of the week for me. I am always excited to see who will be there. It is a strange thing to all of us...we wonder how it works... but in all of the times we have been meeting together, in any of our times together, social or at the church...we have never had the same identical group twice. Our family grows and grows and we do not get into any rut, and we are not some click forming this unique little private group, but we are growing and changing and being blessed in the midst of our gift of singleness.

We are challenged by each other to move forward and if necessary, we help each other get into the car...sometimes we have aches and pains and getting in and out of the car is a chore, but we are willing to come along side and assist each other in times of need. We have times when we do need to get away for reflection and a time of getting a new perspective, but hopefully we will return for encouragement and guidance for the next stage of the journey. It is hard to do the driving sometimes, so we change off drivers and that works for us.

We are praying for a bus...we need one to help us get to the places we want to go...and we want to go together!

We had our own Celebrate 2000 Party! We sent ourselves notes about how we desired to grow in the upcoming year. We sealed them, put them in self-addressed envelopes and in July, I mailed them to each person who was at the party. Some of us, didn't remember making the list, or where we made the list... one fellow, Tanner...thought to himself, "Whoever wrote this about me, sure does know me well." This gives you a flavor and sampling of what fun we have...we laugh at each other and we laugh at ourselves. We hurt and grieve together and we minister together and to others. We sometimes choose to get out of our cars...and join the others already in the van. When we take a trip we do it with lunch and laughter.

Pain in the Journey! → → → → → → → → → →

Facing the pain, is like driving in the rain...you have to be cautious, you have to avoid any sudden stops, or sudden curves. We need to be careful of our speed. When the rain stops, the world seems like a fresh new place...Loss and Grief...passes, we are left with a new perspective and we can drive safely on our way to our destination. The streets have been washed clean. Tears have a way of releasing our emotions and laughter and joy soon follow.

The Singles Ministry in my Church has brought a great sense of peacefulness to my heart and life. It is a lift for me to be with them and to have them pray out loud for me and my little world. I love them deeply.

When I return from my retreats and I join them on Sunday or on Free Fridays...I feel safe. I am loved and cared for by some of the neatest people I have ever met. These are my new friends. I know that their journey up to this point has had some rough roads...but the new course is one that we share and we always carry plenty of snacks and the joy flows.

My children used to sing this little song as we traveled down the road...

"Come and Go with me...to my Father's house...to my Father's house...to my Father's House,

Come and Go with me...to my Father's house, where there is Joy, Joy, Joy."

WORTHY EVENTS TO REMEMBER ALONG THE WAY...

1. Singleness can be very devastating. You may not be a single person, but have you looked around your circle of friends? Do you call a single friend to join you in some of your little trips or times when you do lunch? Do you include some singles over for your holidays, picnics...or times around the pool? I hope so.

2. Did you as a single person ever use any of the tools in your Survival Kit? Why not? What has helped you through the difficult days of grieving and loss? If you are not single, maybe you could encourage your single friends to discover the tools in the Survival Kit?

3. Pray for the Singles Ministry in your church. Discover some ways you might help a widow or a single parent with practical gifts of service. What would be some of those things you could do? When will you get started? Who will you ask to join you as you minister to others? Would you consider starting a program of helping others in your church or even starting a singles ministry? It could be a real turning point in your journey!

4. What part of being single robs you most of your joy? Ask others to pray for you and to come along side of you. This bold disclosure of yourself will defuse the hold the enemy has in this area of your life. Where the light shines on the path...the darkness has to flee.

Single People often feel like
the Invisible People of the Church

Chapter Three

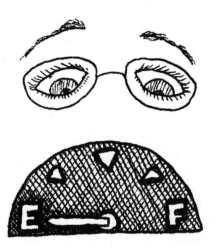

WE'RE ON THE ROAD...

WE COULD BE RUNNING ON EMPTY!

April 19, 1999...was a day when I thought the tank was almost dry. It felt like my energy had been drained...and no one seemed to be replacing the fuel. It occurred to me, that I might need a new fuel pump...Like Right Now!

Heart Attacks happen but to other people! Exactly what I thought! I had watched Bill suffer through several heart attacks, as well as observing his surgery for clogged arteries. I had watched friends and family have heart attacks...but I thought I didn't have time to have a heart attack. The **E...had to mean something else...not empty!**

Will Someone Direct me to the Gas Station? → → → →

Most of the time we watch the gauge on the tank checking to see if we need to find a gas station. I went to the Doctor in September, 1998. I told the Doctor at that time I was not feeling well. My energy level was low...I was tired in the morning after a good night's sleep. I had some times of shortness of breath after mowing my lawn. I also noticed, I felt light headed like I might pass out. He told me to take it easy, not do so much and see how I felt in six months. I was not feeling well in October, and in November, I thought I had the flu...I stayed in bed for 3 days and confessed every sin I knew...prayed and asked God to heal me.

My little episodes were precursors for my up-coming heart attack. Several other episodes occurred and the Doctor just said, it sounded like the flu to him, "drink more fluids and take it easy." If I wasn't better in a few days, call. I did get better, so I didn't call.

When we experience a major upset in our lives by way of a health problem, it causes us to be very cautious for a long time. We ask questions and then we hopefully move on to the next stage. I have been totally healed in the sense that I do not experience major heart problems every day. I do take medication and I am following my new Doctor's instructions. I am on Lopressor, which is a medication for my heart and I do watch what I eat. I avoid red meat and watch the cholesterol intake every day. I take Lipitor and a baby aspirin. I also take an interest in the fat content of all foods. I am working with these two monitors in my life. Eat less, Exercise more...and No Fat, No Cholesterol. I am walking three times a week for twenty minutes. This may not be what your Doctor prescribes but for me...this is my personal roadmap!

Mom and I were recently in the store...she commented she would like some good ice cream...by that I knew she meant, she was going to get regular ice cream. I don't do anything with high fat content...and she often eats with me...and I eat at her house.

She got her ice cream and I got mine. She said, "What kind did you get? I said very proudly, "NO FAT, NO CHOLESTEROL!" She jumped right in with, "NO GOOD!" She doesn't miss a beat!

We do have times when we need to get more gas...we have problems with the car...we have problems with our bodies and with our lives. Where do we run? Who is our resource?

One day I was out mowing my Mom's lawn...the next moment I had a serious heart attack...and my whole life changed. I see every day as a gift. My focus for every day is my life has to be in tune with my Heavenly Father. I am trying to be in close fellowship with Him...through knowing His Son, Jesus. I have placed my faith and trust in Him for my salvation and for my daily needs...I am needy...I admit it. Without Him, I can do nothing.

I read recently, 250,000 people have heart attacks each day, 150,000 die from those heart attacks. I just see life from such a different perspective. I am alive...and I am well!

I look at the gauge and I think to myself...Fill me up...I have a few more miles to go.

Matthew 11:28-30

Then Jesus said, "Come to me, all of you who are weary and carry heavy burdens, and I will give you rest. Take my yoke upon you. Let me teach you, because I am humble and gentle, and you will find rest for your souls. For my yoke fits perfectly, and the burden I give you is light."

Fill my Tank Up with the Premium! → → → → → →

When we come to the end of what has been working for us, we are forced to think about a new plan. My tank needed the best. I had neglected my personal needs. I have been eating for comfort and putting on the weight...which I didn't need. I didn't think about ever being sick. I had lived with someone who had been very sick for a very long time, my little aches and pains seemed like nothing. I neglected me...and I neglected eating and doing the right things for my body. As a result, I was facing a serious wake up call...NOW...I do the best I can...all the time!

The Physical Warning Signs...were not being obeyed or observed by me. I was not paying attention and found myself in a place where I didn't know where the next gas station could be found and I had no knowledge I needed one. I had neglected looking at the gauge. We are not always able to heed the warning signs necessary to change our course for healthier lives. We are not always aware of the changes we need to incorporate into our lives for spiritual maintenance either. We can neglect these areas of our lives because we are living in denial and confusion.

I have a little personal goal planning sheet that works for me...

▽ Adjust my eating according to the goal of being a healthy me.

▽ Adjust my time in the Word to maintain the goal of walking in the Spirit and walking for health.

▽ Be honest with myself and with God.

▽ Communicate with the Lord and with others on a regular basis and listen, too. Communicate with my friends and neighbors on a regular basis.

▽ Discipline in exercise and getting out of my comfort zone. Discipline when it comes to getting rest, etc, so I can attend Church and have time for ministering to others.

▽ Look at my schedule and adjust my time.

▽ If my home and surroundings are in chaos my life will be in disarray. I cannot maintain my home and do ministry at the same time. It is impossible.

▽ Remember to have fun...and be spontaneous. Laughter is healing. Hang out with those who know how to fill up the tank.

▽ Look at each day as a gift from God.

I used to think if I devoted too much time to **me**, I was probably not caring for others. In the year of 2000...my verses for the year were chosen back in December...and for that entire year the verses were exactly what I needed to help me grow in the area of my life of knowing that nothing can happen to me outside of the will of God.

Ecclesiastes 3:11-15

God had made everything beautiful for its own time. He has planted eternity in the human heart, but even so, people cannot see the whole scope of God's work from beginning to end. So I concluded that there is nothing better for people than to be happy and to enjoy themselves as long as they can. And people should eat and drink and enjoy the fruits of their labor, for these are gifts from God.

Other verses have been meaningful to me along the way.

Ecclesiastes 5:19-20

And it is a good thing to receive wealth from God and the good health to enjoy it. To enjoy your work and accept your lot in life—that is indeed a gift from God. People who do this rarely look with sorrow on the past, for God has given them reasons for joy.

Regular Maintenance and Check-Ups... → → → → →

I have to maintain my body...but I also need to be responsible when it comes to being spiritually healthy as well. A retreat of silence is a good goal for my life and I am sure it could benefit you as well.

It is all about getting away at different times and spending the time in prayer, reading the scriptures, and writing in my journal. Setting goals...being quiet before the Lord...or spending a day fasting and praying. These disciplines are part of the maintenance of a busy person who wants to serve the Lord.

I have to find time for the check-up and for the maintenance if I am to serve with energy and freshness...otherwise, I become dull and listless. Your spiritual check up may look different from mine just as my physical check up may look different from yours. Sometimes when I take my car in for a check-up it requires action. I have to get a new part or have something checked. I have to do what the mechanic says. David is the mechanic and my neighbor...and he knows what is best for my car...that is his job. We seek Spiritual expertise when we need to look at our Spiritual Growth process.

Usually when I have something wrong with my car, I run it past my son who is also a mechanic. Tim can repair most anything. Do you have a person in your life that you run your spiritual needs by...just for clarification or affirmation? It is important to have people in our lives who can and will assist us in our maintenance and check-up areas.

Let's face it...we are the drivers and we are the ones in the car...and we should be the first to recognize when something is wrong. We are also aware when something in our Spiritual life is not right. Keep short books with God...and do not allow things to pile up...it can cost a great deal in the long haul. If we neglect the red light on the dash...it can cost a great deal if left without inspection and unchecked.

When my car doesn't start well...it may be jerky or it starts to use more gas...I know I have a situation that requires my full attention. When it is time for my Spiritual tune up, I notice it too, I become irritable and grouchy. I have little or no patience for what is going on around me. I am not planning well and I am using poor judgement. I make hasty decisions without seeking counsel. I know I can't do anything on my own to maintain my position with the Lord concerning my salvation... but I can certainly check in when my tank starts needing some more fuel.

I am really thinking in terms of my fellowship with my Heavenly Father, and my personal on-going relationship with the Father. Living my life as much as it is possible with me: I have to start by confessing sin, and trying to walk in the power of the Holy Spirit. I need to be filled with the Holy Spirit. I want to walk in fellowship with Him, and that can only happen when I keep my relationship with God honest. When I quench the Holy Spirit by walking with unconfessed sin present, I am not in fellowship. My Salvation cannot be touched but my friendship with God is broken by sin.

James 4:17

Remember, it is sin to know what we ought to do and then not do it.

Ephesians 5:15-20

So be careful how you live, not as fools but as those who are wise. Make the most of every opportunity for doing good in these evil days. Don't act thoughtlessly, but try to understand what the Lord wants you to do. Don't be drunk with wine, because that will ruin your life. Instead, let the Holy Spirit fill and control you. Then you will sing psalms and hymns and spiritual songs among yourselves, making music to the Lord in your hearts. And you will always give thanks for everything to God the Father in the name of our Lord Jesus Christ.

Tuning and filling are two different distinct actions...but when I am tuned into the will of God, I will be seeking times of filling without waiting until I run dry.

1 John 5:18

We know that those who have become part of God's family do not make a practice of sinning, for God's Son holds them securely, and the evil one cannot get his hands on them.

1 John 5:21

Dear children, keep away from anything that might take God's place in your hearts.

Last Chance...You Need to Fill up Now!

I have asked myself many times, why do I put off doing what I know I must do. **E...means Empty in any language and I had better take notice.**

Why do we wait and procrastinate? We often get into being last minute, *fly-by-our-seats people*, because we do not make a plan. When we plan a trip, we need to think about where we will be when we need to get the tank filled up. I used to hate to travel over some areas of the wide open spaces and the desolate areas of Minnesota. There is a stretch from Bemidiji to Duluth which is almost nothing but swamp and trees. I never wanted to travel over that stretch of county alone, or even with the tank half full, because there just wasn't anything out there to help if you ran out of gas. I am so grateful for the mobile phone. I don't use it a lot, but if you need to connect with someone for help it is good to know it is available.

Who do you call, where do you go for help?

Ephesians 3:14-21

When I think of the wisdom and scope of God's plan, I fall to my knees and pray to the Father, the Creator of everything in heaven and on earth. I pray that from His glorious, unlimited resources He will give you mighty inner strength through His Holy Spirit. And I pray that Christ will be more and more at home in your hearts as you trust in Him. May your roots go down deep into the soil of God's marvelous love. And may you have the power to understand, as all God's people should, how wide, how long, how high, and how deep his love really is. May you experience the love of Christ, though it is so great you will never fully understand it. Then you will be filled with the fullness of life and power that comes from God.

Now glory be to God! By His mighty power at work within us, He is able to accomplish infinitely more than we would ever dare to ask or hope. May He be given glory in the church and in Christ Jesus forever and ever through endless ages. Amen.

Sunday Morning Worship is a highlight of my week...but I cannot go all week on just one hour of being with the Lord and other believers. Worship and fellowship with other believers is like getting a full tank of spiritual fuel. It is not a substitute for me spending time in the word, praying and relating to the Father one to one. Someone else can fill up their tank, but it will not effect me and my tank. We cannot rely on how others are choosing to live their lives...filling their tanks and doing their maintenance...we have to make sure we are doing what is right for us and what is pleasing to the Lord.

Ephesians 5:10

Try to find out what is pleasing to the Lord.

One size fits all doesn't always apply. Our relationship with the Lord is based on our individual relationship with Him. I know that in the manual for cars you can read...based upon certain road tests, etc. this model will require maintenance to be done when you have driven so many miles. It is a general statement and in a lot of situations it really does apply to many cars. I also know, we are not cars...God says, "We are fearfully and wonderfully made." He has a plan for you and for me.

God gives us guidelines for our personal lives. We must as individuals choose to trust in Him and follow Him. We each have our own set of plans. Yes, it is true...if we follow His plan in full obedience to His plan we will be blessed, and if we do not...we will reap what we sow. It is called cause and effect. God's word is generic. It is for all of us, and still we have our own path.

I may need to get my tank filled on a daily basis whereas, you might be able to go for a couple of days without filling yours. We run into real trouble when we start comparing ourselves with one another and thinking we have a tested formula that works for everyone. I have tried to clearly state, that some of the things I am suggesting have worked for me...these are truths I have found to be helpful for me, but I do not know your total situation and I do not know what God is doing in your life. I need to trust in God and so do you. I need to believe His plan for me, and you need to trust Him for His will in your life.

Ephesians 5:1-2

Follow God's example in everything you do, because you are His dear children. Live a life filled with love for others, following the example of Christ, who loved you and gave Himself as a sacrifice to take away your sins. And God was pleased, because that sacrifice was like sweet perfume to Him.

Be Careful Where You Take Your Car. → → → → → →

When I moved here in the O'Fallon area, I was careful to find someone I could trust to inspect and look after my car. I was fortunate to find my neighbor Dave. He had a family business that serviced cars...and I needed this kind of person in my life to help with the maintenance of my little Dodge Spirit. I found a convenient and safe place. One day, I had a major problem...I had a flat tire. This is major for me...so I drove down the street and he repaired it for me. I do believe I received special attention, in fact, I know I did. It helps to know the owners and it helps to have a safe place to get your car checked and to have the proper maintenance and repairs done on the spot.

It is a real blessing to me to have a church home. It is a place I can attend where I feel cared for and nurtured. Church attendance will not guarantee your place in heaven, but worship and fellowship is very important in doing the Spiritual maintenance. I think we must first of all, go to the place where God has called us to go. I asked the Lord long before I moved back to the St. Louis area to help me find a really good church...a place where I could give my gifts to that body and where they could give their gifts to me. I knew I would need a lot of building up.

I would be a stranger and I needed a place to feel safe. We spend a lot of time looking for our homes and I think we should spend time praying and thinking about how important it is to find just the right church. We make choices based upon our need for a home...a good school district, living close to our job, or a good shopping area...why not take that much care in finding our church home? Finding a place where we will be able to serve and where we will receive sound teaching. It is necessary if we are to grow and mature.

I Neglected My Physical Needs! → → → → → → → →

My heart attack lasted a few hours. I was put on medication, I was placed in the ICU unit, I was given 24 hour care. I was put on oxygen...so many things being monitored while I was in the hospital. It happened so quickly. I was not expecting it, I had not checked out a doctor, I had not checked out the hospital, or how quick the response would be from a 911 call. God provided for me in my time of dire need. God was always looking over me. He provided the place for me to be when I needed fuel and energy for my tank. He wants to provide for you even though you may not feel any need of him at this time. He really cares about you. You are going to need his services and you had better start to check out the situation. How is it with your soul?

I had forgotten a major part of my life...my physical needs... but God still cared for me. He never neglected my care or his concern for me. I am amazed at how many ways we have to trust God.

James 4:10

When you bow down before the Lord and admit your dependence on Him, He will lift you up and give you honor.

1 Peter 5:8-9a

Be careful! Watch out for attacks from the Devil, your great enemy. He prowls around like a roaring lion, looking for some victim to devour. Take a firm stand against him, and be strong in your faith.

Do the maintenance...and count the cost. Following Christ is the only thing that counts. Find out where the nearest watering hole is...and don't stray far from it. Always seek out fellowship and a place where you can be rejuvenated and refreshed.

WORTHY EVENTS TO REMEMBER ALONG THE WAY...

1. When was the last time you took a spiritual inventory of your personal walk with the Lord?

2. What kinds of things are happening in your life today that may indicate you are running around with your tank half empty?

3. Have you considered getting away and doing a Retreat of Silence? It can replenish your tank and energize you for the next adventure. Have you considered telling another person you are feeling overwhelmed...ask for prayer. It is a good and healthy thing to be able to admit you need help.

4. If you are not in a safe place in your fellowship, seek a safe place...a place where you can be encouraged and where you will have people in your life to hold you accountable and grow with you. You may need to pray for those who care for your soul...ask God to help your leaders and give them wisdom as they shepherd the flock.

5. If you had symptoms of a heart attack...would you act? Or would you put it off and deny the symptoms? If you are not doing well in your walk with the Lord, are you going to deny the problem and put it off...how long?

It says if we want to have fellowship with him, we are to:

1 John 1:9-10

But if we confess our sins to Him, He is faithful and just to forgive us and to cleanse us from every wrong. If we claim we have not sinned, we are calling God a liar and showing that his word has no place in our hearts.

Restoration and repair is the work of the Holy Spirit. He wants to totally restore us and our walk with our Heavenly Father. I pray that today, we may all find our refreshment and strength in Him.

Chapter Four

WE'RE ON THE ROAD...

WITH AGING PARENTS AND ACTIVE GRANDCHILDREN!

We talk a lot about how our lives change...the passengers agree:

I enjoy taking trips when Mom is traveling with me...she packs little lunches. We used to be able to eat egg salad sandwiches...and little tuna sandwiches...but because of the cholesterol, we pack different kinds of lunches as we travel to our destinations. Change is always part of the trip. We get lost and we find ourselves, we sing and we read maps and signs... it is always an adventure.

When you travel with the grandchildren...they know where the fast food places are and they really know where the Krispy Kreme Doughnut Co. is...and it is only a few blocks from my home...that is a pleasant short trip they like to take.

Josh, my grandson knew the roads to and from Duluth to St. Louis. I was glad to have him with me in the car when I moved from Cloquet to St. Louis...he was my guiding map. He watched me cry as I drove down the road and left the last place where I had lived with his Grandpa.

Going down the road with parents and children is a tremendous trip. We each bring a certain set of concerns and desires as we travel. We may have to stop for the grandparents and the children and it can be disruptive to the plan...until we come to understand, they *are* the plan.

What Does it Mean to be a Caregiver?

> *Sometimes I honestly wonder whom is taking care of whom? My Mom is in good health for someone who is 90 years old. She always reminds me, "I know what it is like to be 65, but you don't know what it is like to be 90."*

When we become caregivers...the roles change.

One day Mom and I were walking on the parking lot as we were headed to the store. I reached out for her to take my hand...and she reminded me that years ago, she used to reach out for my hand and walk with me so she could look out for traffic and lead the way. The roles have reversed.

We must adjust to these new roles. It is not easy. We have to view our parents in a different way.

I know my children are watching how I care for their Granny... perhaps, as they watch the process, they will learn how to care for me.

I found some helpful tools in the survival manual. It addresses the issues of how to care for our aging parents.

1. Allow them to be part of the decision-making as it relates to their lives.

2. Help them, but do not take over. Allow them to have something to do for themselves that is part of taking care of themselves. It gives them dignity and they need the stimulation of making their own decisions.

3. Encourage them to do the things they used to enjoy. Make it possible for them to still be able to do those things on a smaller scale. My Mom used to garden big time...now she has pots of plants and a few tomatoes and a few peppers. It is fun for her and it does not tire her out. She plants the seeds for our tomato plants. We order the seeds together from the seed catalogues and it reminds her of the days when she and my dad used to plant a huge garden.

4. Help them to stay on track with medications, etc. Find out what they are taking, why they are taking it...and work with the doctor in dealing with their health issues. We have a nurse in our church and she cares for all of us...as a Parish Nurse. I can ask Bernice about any health issues and she has been very helpful to me. She and I observe Mom together and she encourages me regarding Mom and her health problems. Do not be afraid to ask others to help you with issues you may not understand.

5. As much as it is possible, review with your parents on a weekly basis what is happening in their lives. My Mom and I have set times to be together. We try and shop together, go to church together and we have some meals together. When I am traveling, I have helpers to cover for me...they take my Mom to church, or to the store...or call and check in on her while I am gone. This helps me to focus while I am away and it gives her confidence that someone will be checking in on her on a daily basis. My children often help with these items as well. It is important to keep a routine for our parents, but every now and then we should do something fun and spontaneous with them as well. It forces them to get out of their routines and they have to act quickly. *"It sharpens the pencil,"* as we say.

One of the things we must remember in being the caregiver for our parents...our children will be watching how we do it and they will use our modeling for their example. I want to make sure my sons see the right kinds of things. I have stated this several times, but I do not think it can be overstated. I lose patience sometimes with my role, because it is hard and because I am afraid of the alternatives. Thus far, my Mom's health is very good and we rejoice in her good health, but we know all of our days are numbered. Mom and I have discussed her health issues many times. We are together thanking God for each of her days.

When the parents move into your home, it is not simple. Your parents have had the role of taking care of you as you grew up in their home, and now you are grown and they are living in your home. The roles have reversed and it is not an easy concept to live with on a daily basis.

It can cause conflict and partly I think it is due to not knowing exactly what the healthy boundaries must be in this situation. Parents and children...need to rely upon the Lord, His guidance and wise counsel. It is not about being easy, but relying upon the Lord to give grace and understanding.

It is important that you establish the healthy boundaries. You cannot meet all of your parents' needs. They often have difficulty because they have feelings of little worth. They have lost their definition of meaning and purpose. We need to help them redefine their roles and purpose. This takes some serious thought...It is important that we come together and decide what things they can do around the house and how you can mutually serve and help one another in the new roles. One parent I know did the dishes, it was her responsibility and the grandchildren were assigned to different tasks...the children loved it. One day the Grandparent was tired...and told them, "we're eating out of paper plates today, and it's not a picnic." Humor will carry you through a lot of difficult times. It is necessary to adjust your behaviors, flexibility has to be the bottom line. Give and take...parents...cannot be rigid with their children, and children cannot be rigid with their parents. Get away from the situation every now and then. You need to have some free time, you will be better for it...and you can start with a new slate of energy for the task when you come back to the family unit. Caregiving requires relying upon the strength that God provides...always!

1 Peter 4:10-11

*God has given gifts to each of you from his great variety of spiritual gifts. Manage them well so that God's generosity can flow through you. Are you called to be a speaker? Then speak as though God himself were speaking through you. **Are you called to help others? Do it with all the strength and energy that God supplies.** Then God will be given glory in everything through Jesus Christ. All glory and power belong to Him forever and ever. Amen.*

Grandparents Often Become the Main Caregivers for Grandchildren. → → → → → → → → → → → →

It is happening more and more in our society. Single Parents need the help of their parents in caring and nurturing their children. Often the grandparents have custody of the grandchildren. The family unit takes on a different look from the traditional family unit. We have to face this change and adjust to how we deal with the changing family unit. It requires flexing and adjusting. It also takes a lot of energy.

Parents have raised their children and now they are raising another family. I admire grandparents who have the stamina and energy for this calling. There can be a great deal of pain in this family adjustment, and for that reason, great care must be given in helping the child feel loved and cared for during this change from traditional to a well-balanced working family unit. **We need to pray for those we know who have the grandchildren in the car while going down the road.**

I have observed the changing family for several years. My

concerns stem from seeing children at times being lost in the shuffle while others seemingly thrive. My concern is that as a caring Church family, we need to come along side and support these newly defined families. We can help by praying and even practical gifts of helping hands. Jesus came from a blended family and we need to be considerate of those in this situation and not judgmental. I grieve for the families in turmoil during this process. I am sure it is not one they would have chosen but this is where they are and we need to address the issues with kindness and love.

▽ Children need to feel loved and safe.

▽ Grandparents need a second wind for the task.

▽ The Church Family needs to extend survival tools for the situation along with acceptance.

▽ Grandparents make sacrifices and they need help as they do it again.

▽ The enemy could use this as a hotbed for jealousy, anger, shame and blame.

Proverbs 19:20-21

Get all the advice and instruction you can, and be wise the rest of your life. You can make many plans, but the LORD's purpose will prevail.

We need to be extremely careful how we view others and give grace and genuine love to all families. It is not an easy task to raise children and then raise them again.

The world offers resources for helping families who are caring for their children's children...but we as a church really need to offer support and help for families who are dealing with this stressful family situation, as well.

▽ Families could meet together once a month and share helpful suggestions as to how they are coping. Often legal action has to be taken, and dealing with the legal aspect of this difficult situation requires patience and help. Some families work it out with little or no snags, but other families have years of torment and friction because of the legalities and rights. Not an easy place to be when children are waiting in the wings to be cared for and helped through the confusion of this childhood experience.

In our churches today, we need to be tuned into assisting and providing support and tools for surviving the challenge of the changing role of the family. Often others who are caring for their grandchildren come along side with help and encouragement. This can be done without a formal program...but if we are to look around in our communities, we might want to offer this help to others as we attempt to be salt and light where we live. Our Churches could set the pace and offer Godly assistance and encouragement. We could develop programs that would indeed come along side and assist families during this adjustment period...of surviving in their new situations.

I have often observed if we are to serve others, we must meet them where they hurt!

If the grandparents are raising the grandchild and the parent is still in the picture, you can have another set of dynamics. Who disciplines the child, who provides for the child? The parent may be like a revolving door, coming and going and doing the disappearing act from time to time. This causes confusion for the child. It is important to establish the chain of command and exactly how the roles of the family will work in this new environment.

▽ Children need structure and freedom...children need to know who is going to be there when they come home from school, who will hold them accountable and who will look in the book bag and help them make decisions about what book they should make their book report on for the up-coming semester. Children really do thrive in safe environments, with people who will consistently be there on a day-to-day basis.

As we are driving down the road we have many *kinds of people and situations going on...in the car and outside of the window.* We as the church can no longer dismiss this part of our body as being unnecessary or not valid. We must as the church come along side of these families who are part of us on Sunday Mornings. How can we offer help to those caring for the elderly parent...and for those families who are caring for their grandchildren? We must band together and be committed to serving and helping one another. The first step might be in just acknowledging that these people are sitting in our pews, and then offering support and tools with real life (Come Along Side–practical help). Our concerns for those in our pews could be a very good turning point in our **body life** experience.

My family is personally touched by both of these situations and as I view them and am part of them I see the church as having a golden opportunity to do good to those in the household of faith. I understand for myself, if the body of Christ needs support and help in these areas how much more do those who are pre-Christians need this kind of caring concern. My neighbors, and friends are dealing with these very same issues, how do they cope, who do they turn to...and is God their resource? I can only assume how difficult these issues might be, but it is a golden opportunity for the Church to practice doing what we know needs to be done. It is making the practical application of the scriptures to love others and accept them where they are living. Getting out there beyond our own little Christian Ghetto...offering kindness and affirmation can be what we often refer to as Lifestyle Evangelism.

Galatians 6:10

Whenever we have the opportunity, we should do good to everyone, especially to our Christian brothers and sisters.

James 4:17

Remember, it is sin to know what you ought to do and then not do it.

Proverbs 25:11

Timely advice is as lovely as golden apples in a silver basket.

Two things we need in our lives, to be wise and to listen to wisdom. We will be blessed when we care for others and come along side of those who are caring for their loved ones. We need wise counsel but often do not seek it from the Lord or from our Church. I pray we might be people who share good things with those in the household of faith...and those we are seeking to lead to Christ.

WORTHY EVENTS TO REMEMBER ALONG THE WAY...

1. How could you personally support or encourage someone who is caring for their elderly parent?

   When might you do that act of kindness?

2. If you are a member of a small church you may not know anyone who is raising their grandchild, but you may know someone in your neighborhood. What kindness could you do in that situation?

3. You may identify with one of these families. Is it possible you could start a support group for others who are living where you are living? It may take courage and it is a risk, but others are in need of hearing how you are coping and what tools you have discovered along the way.

4. Who is riding in your car now? Who may be riding in your car 15 years from now? Perhaps, God is preparing you to be ready should this need come to your family.

   James 4:10

   When you bow down before the Lord and admit your dependence on Him, He will lift you up and give you honor.

   We cannot do it on our own...our journey is far too complicated and the road is sometimes slick from the rain or snow... ask God to give you strength as you strive to obey and follow His leading in your life. Caring for others is not an easy task. We need to pray and support one another as we strive to please Him while running to and from our cars, or just driving to the store...caring for those whom God has given to us takes energy and obedience.

5. Would you choose this aspect of family life? Caregivers are in the car...and they need support as well.

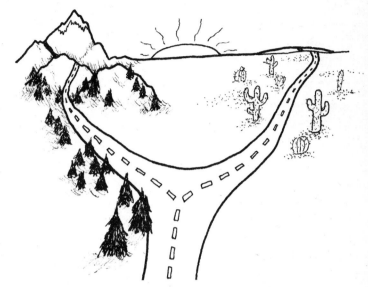

CHAPTER FIVE

WE'RE ON THE ROAD...

WITH DECISIONS AND BACK SEAT DRIVERS!

Some of us are dealing with a crossroad in our lives. We are wondering, what is next? What will we be doing tomorrow, or next week? We ponder and we assume. Being in the will of God takes a lot of prayer and waiting upon the Lord for His guidance and leadership. Some of us have been sitting in the drive-way for a long time. The car is actually starting to rust... the tires are almost out of air, and the license plate is definitely out of date. WE CAN'T DECIDE WHAT TO DO...so we do nothing.

Others of us...are in the car, but in the back seat giving directions to the driver...but the driver is not having any of it and reminds us that we are only passengers and they know exactly where they are going. We are at the crossroad doubting all of it. We have problems with authority figures and we have problems with following directions. We want to be in the front seat and are assured by our delusional thinking that we need to be in the front seat because we deserve it. We develop the skill of being complainers and whiners which can in time become so uncomfortable for those around us, they tell us we are not allowed to come along, even for the ride.

What Determines the Direction? ➔ ➔ ➔ ➔ ➔ ➔ ➔ ➔

The view from the rear seat is not what we want to see...but it beats looking at life through the rear view mirror...still it is not driving...and it is not sitting in the front seat.

Families with children understand this concept perfectly...We're in the car and heading off for an adventure...the discussion relates to who will ride in the front seat? "So and so, rode up front last time." "Yes, but he is being disciplined and now it is my turn." Sometimes, deciding this very important position can take three or four minutes...meanwhile, no one else can take their seat because jockeying for position is part of the travel experience...who will get the best seat? Who deserves the best seat? This doesn't happen when both parents are traveling on the excursion... the parents will be in the front seats unless Mom rides in the back with a new baby. It is a matter of settling the question of what is fair and who will ride in the important seat?

Why do we react in such negative ways about position and fairness? I am an only child...that hasn't changed...I always sat in the back seat. I was blessed because we had a car. I became accustomed to the back seat and as long as I was in the car...I didn't care. A lot of discussion is given to the topic of *one* child, and how spoiled they can be...which can be true, but one thing for sure, if you are the *only* child...you always know exactly where you will sit.

The seat where we are in the car often determines how we make decisions. If we are driving, we had better know where we are going. We had better be able to read the gas gauge and the dial that indicates the speed. I can be aware of several routes to my destination, and all of them will finally take me to my destination, but I do have to decide which one I will take. I can only take one route at a time. I can only do one thing at a time. If I am in the back seat, I had better choose to be with someone who is going my way. Sitting in the back seat can be a time for observing, for when we do get to sit in the front seat...hopefully we will appreciate the responsibility of being in the driver's seat.

Determining the Will of God? → → → → → → → →

There are some issues that interfere with knowing the will of God. I call them detours....routes that take us from the main road. It can be due to repairs, and the road needs to take a different direction...but if we stay on the detour we will never get back to the main route.

OUR WAY → → → → → → →	GOD'S WILL
Complaining	Contentment
Compromise	Courage
Competition	Confidence
Complacency	Conviction
Conflict	Cooperation
Control	Consistent
Confusion	Charity
Coveting	Commitment

These are issues that keep us unsettled and caught up in the detour. We wonder around missing our opportunities and feeling left out of the circle. God has a plan...God has a path and He wants to come along side of us during this process as we surrender to His will.

Joshua 1:9 NIV

Have I not commanded you? Be strong and courageous.

Do not be terrified, do not be discouraged, for the LORD your God will be with you wherever you go.

Knowing God is what gives us courage.

Job 11:18 NIV

You will be secure, because there is hope; you will look about you and take rest in safety.

God will give you courage when you are afraid.

Deuteronomy 20:1b

The LORD your God...is with you!

Isaiah 41:10

Don't be afraid, for I am with you. Do not be dismayed, for I am your God. I will strengthen you. I will help you. I will uphold you with my victorious right hand.

When I am lost and need directions, I usually am faced with the reality of **Correction:**

 God allows obstacles in our path so we will learn to trust in Him and Him alone. **We're not in control.**

We are so prone to follow our own path and our own sense of what we think will work. We are bent on self-destruction at times...wanting our own will over the will of God which brings peace and contentment. We fall into the Control Trap... and we are going to have it our way...because we have become comfortable with being in the driver's seat. We are not happy in any other position. We want our good ole Comfort Zone... and we fight or take flight if we do not get our way!

Ephesians 2:8-10

God saved you by His special favor when you believed. And you can't take credit for this; it is a gift from God. Salvation is not a reward for the good things we have done, so none of us can boast about it. For we are God's masterpiece. He has created us anew in Christ Jesus, so that we can do the good things He planned for us long ago.

He has good things planned for us to do...His will.

Isaiah 29:24

Those in error will then believe the truth, and those who constantly complain will accept instruction.

 God has a way of **correcting** our path and leading us to know and understand...His will.

Hebrews 4:14-16

That is why we have a great High Priest who has gone to heaven. Jesus the Son of God. Let us cling to Him and never stop trusting Him. This High Priest of ours understands our weaknesses, for He faced all of the same temptations we do, yet He did not sin. So let us come boldly to the throne of our gracious God. There we will receive His mercy, and we will find grace to help us when we need it.

When we feel like we are wandering and lost, we can seek Him, or not! His will is not unreasonable...in truth, we find peace and perspective when we yield our will to His. We stumble and we finally find the right direction and it is the only path we want to be on...it doesn't matter as long as we are in the car. Often our pride and stubbornness keeps us from being in fellowship with God and on the road of obedience. The will of God is after all, doing what he has called us to do.

Romans 12:1-2

And so, dear Christian friends, I plead with you to give your bodies to God. Let them be a living and holy sacrifice—the kind He will accept. When you think of what He has done for you, is this too much to ask? Don't copy the behavior and customs of this world, but let God transform you into a new person by changing the way you think. Then you will know what God wants you to do, and you will know how good and pleasing and perfect His will really is.

"And you will know how good and pleasing and perfect His will really is."

We do harm to ourselves by demanding our own way. We want to be in control, we want to be the ones to give the directions and set the course. We think because we have been given the responsibility of being the driver...or the back-seat driver we know it all, and we want to make sure that everyone is well aware of our authority. We take charge because the alternative would be relying upon the Lord and because we are not sure what that would be about...*we take charge... because we can't really trust anyone.*

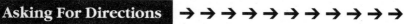 **As the driver, we need to know where we are going...but we also need to check the road map and trust God to help us along the way.**

God often is helping us define our true character by taking us through valleys and rocky roads. The will of God is not always the smoothest route nor the most direct. We may have to take a detour now and then...because it helps us to appreciate the main road.

Asking For Directions → → → → → → → → → →

I personally hate to ask for directions...my husband did ask for directions, but very seldom did he have to ask because he was prepared. He would have a map of any state we were traveling through in the glove compartment of the car. When we moved into the high tech age, he would have the directions all clearly written out from the Motor Club...today he would be using the Internet...he was ready for any imaginable probable disruption to our planned course. We still could get lost, and meet unforeseen obstacles along the way, in spite of his efforts to prevent problems. We cannot totally, always, be prepared...but as much as it is possible within us...we should seek directions...and then expect to learn how to walk by faith.

Many of us think we have it all figured out? How does that kind of thinking promote, "walking by faith and not by sight?" We need to learn to ask our Heavenly Father just exactly what road we are on?..who will be driving?..and to point out to us the historical places along the way! I feel really good when someone prays for me to be on the right path. I find it helpful to ask the Lord...to direct me, and give me assurance that I am on the best path. It gives me a sense of well being. I go to Him...because, *I admit and need, "HELP!"*

Philippians 1:6

And I am sure that God, who began the good work within you, will continue His work until it is finally finished...

I need to know that truth in my heart...long before I even walk out of my house to get into the car...I need to be assured that as I am moving down the path...my Lord will be with me all the time. I need assurance...or I'm not going!

When Nehemiah went back to his homeland to restore the walls...he wanted to be assured of God's leadership and His presence...every step of the way.

Nehemiah 1:10-11

"We are your servants, the people you rescued by your great power and might. O Lord, please hear my prayer! Listen to the prayers of those of us who delight in honoring you. Please grant me success now as I go to ask the king for a great favor. Put it into his heart to be kind to me."

In those days I was the king's cup-bearer.

Nehemiah was asking permission to go and do a work for the Lord...but he still needed God's assurance that He would indeed give him success and the king would grant his request and allow him to return to his homeland to repair the broken down wall.

Nehemiah was indeed granted his desire and when he went back to Jerusalem the condition of the wall was far worse than he had even imagined...his spirit was broken...but because of the situation of the people and the wall, he received strength to do the task. He asked for strength to complete the task of rebuilding the walls...he received the counsel of God for his task.

There were times when he wanted to quit...he had times when his enemies actually made fun of him, taunted him about the foolishness of his task...but he did not waver...God's will should inspire us and call us to go beyond ourselves for total obedience to His will. We need to put God first, above all else we have going on in our lives. When we purposefully put God first...He honors our commitment.

Nehemiah...*prayed...planned...purposed in his heart to do it...and then he persevered!*

Nehemiah 6:15-16

So on October 2, the wall was finally finished—just fifty-two days after we had begun. When our enemies and the surrounding nations heard about it, they were frightened and humiliated. They realized that this work had been done with the help of our God.

When the wall was completed they celebrated...all of Israel celebrated.

Nehemiah 8:10

And Nehemiah continued, "Go and celebrate with a feast of choice foods and sweet drinks, and share gifts of food with people who have nothing prepared. This is a sacred day before our Lord. Don't be dejected and sad, for the joy of the LORD is your strength!"

When we are in the car...and on the path...and we are headed in the right direction...we will have completed the course... and one day, there will be a great celebration. It isn't over yet...we are merely on the road...one day we will reach our final destination and the trip will be completed. We will have finished the race...the course which was set before us...and we will receive our reward. The safest place we can ever be... is in the will of God.

Now, About Those Back-Seat Drivers!

The kind of person you want riding in the back seat is one who may also know the way...someone who can take over the driving if you get tired...someone who can pass you a sandwich if you are hungry...someone who will keep you awake and help read the signs if the person in the front seat falls asleep...someone who has the change for the toll road.

You do not need someone yelling, "Are we in the Mountains Yet?"

> *We decided to take a trip to Maine...my husband was even considering a job transfer...and we decided to make it a vacation trip...and some trip it was. The boys were eager for the mountains because according to the map, they knew we would be closer to our final destination...and over and over again they would ask... "Are we in the mountains yet?" It became a theme and we all wanted to be in the mountains...when we finally did get in the mountains the ascent was so unnoticeable they didn't realize it...and when we were finally in the mountains it was not as they imagined. They couldn't believe we were actually in the mountains.*

Back-seat drivers...can be useful, or they can be complainers and nay sayers! If you see a place to eat, they don't want to eat there...or they may need to stop often because they aren't willing to stop when the others stop. They can even get sick so they have to be put up in the front because they are car sick...it can all be very legitimate.

Back-seat drivers need to remember their roles...and have acceptance for that place and time.!

It's Time to Test Our Abilities...

Some of us need to determine what our role is and then be content in that role until such a time that it may change. My grandson was so eager to drive. He could hardly wait to be a driver. He observed many things about driving...he knew the rules, he watched my son's speed limit which was not always helpful to Tim...but nevertheless, the day came...and he moved from the back-seat driver's position to the driver's position. He had his own car, his own insurance, and his own job to support his position as the driver.

What we observe and learn as a back-seat driver has a strong influence upon us as drivers.

⬣ **W**ill we be **Considerate?**

⬣ **W**ill we be **Responsible?**

⬣ **W**ill we be **Able to Follow Directions?**

⬣ **W**ill we **Observe the Pedestrians?**

Yes, we are in the car...observing the directions and the detours. We're learning to make better decisions...we understand the will of God...and at times, are even willing to be obedient to follow Him. We are especially eager if we see a policemen parked behind a sign observing our driving.

Don't spend too much time sitting in the driveway...life can pass you by if you are too afraid to risk, change, choose, and fail...all of these can happen to me on a daily basis. Living the Christian life is not about being driven around by someone else all the time...it is about getting into the car and going down the road. I didn't learn to drive until I was 27 years old...it was scary for me and for my kids. My husband had tried to help me, but I hit a tree the first time he was in the car with me and so he was not too inclined to help me learn. I finally had to learn to drive on my own.

I had to drive 3 miles every day to the spring to get our drinking water. We lived out in the country and if I waited for Bill to have the time to get the water, we would have no drinking water. I would put my children in the back seat and we would go down the road for three miles to get the water from a spring...turn around and then drive back home. I would practice parking in the driveway, and practice I did. The boys would be really quiet while I was driving... which was very different for them. One day, Michael, the oldest said to the others... "Let's pray for Mom as she drives." This simple prayer carried me many miles. I took them along when it was time to get my driver's license. The instructor said he didn't think we should have them in the car...and I said, "Sir, they will be with me always, so why not now, too?"

I successfully obtained my driver's license on a snowy day in February. My neighbor took me to the town where I was to prove my abilities...it was a risk, I had to change, I had to learn to make choices and I could fail...but God honored me that day and I'm driving over the river and through the woods. I will always remember the road to the spring...simple beginnings take us beyond ourselves.

Ecclesiastes 11:4

If you wait for perfect conditions, you will never get anything done.

WORTHY EVENTS TO REMEMBER ALONG THE WAY...

1. Why do you think we hesitate to ask God for Directions?

2. Do you have times when you feel you are totally lost and unable to read the map? How do you feel during those times? What do you do?

3. Do you see yourself as the driver, God as the driver, or do you see it as God allowing you to be the driver and He is the map?

4. What kind of back seat driver are you? Why?

5. Have you ever considered yourself a "Control Freak?" Does this get in the way of following the path God has for you in your life? How?

Psalm 143:8

Let me hear of your unfailing love to me in the morning, for I am trusting you. Show me where to walk, for I have come to you in prayer.

Psalm 144:15b

Happy indeed are those whose God is the LORD.

Chapter Six

WE'RE ON THE ROAD...

WITH EMERGENCIES AND TROUBLES!

How do We Handle Emergencies and Repairs?

We all know that the rain falls upon the just and the unjust... We sometimes think it is our responsibility to determine for God who will be the just and the unjust. We want grace for our lives but we are not sure we want grace for someone else...especially, if we have decided we don't like that person or their point of view.

Have you found yourself driving down a road and had someone cut you off...or the car ahead of you goes racing by and you think to yourself, "where is a policeman when that person needs to have someone observing his law-breaking actions?" We are so delighted as we are driving further down the road and find the person pulled over by the officer with the little round red light flashing on and off for all of the world to see. They are in big trouble and we are glad...and smiling at the situation. "Ya—na ya—na ya—na."

We feel a strong sense that justice has somehow prevailed. We feel validated. We have no patience for problems, emergencies, or repairs...any disruption to our trip is a crisis.

People used to have a thing about what kind of car they drove. Families were known by the cars or trucks they drove...it had to be a Ford...or a Truck...or for sure a GMC product. Personally, I just wanted my form of transportation to go down the road.

I am very grateful for my son, Tim...he can repair just about anything any car needs. He has spent a great deal of time over the years taking care of the needs of "old cars." He has been known to get a "Junker" and work on it until it was up and running. He might have a missionary buddy coming home from the mission field and in need of a good vehicle during his time of furlough. Tim would repair the old car and it would take the missionaries over the road. Tim has collected many tools over the years and repairs many things...motorcycles, planes, garbage disposals, toasters and garage door openers.

When I lived in Minnesota, I soon learned every thinking person carried a survival kit and some tools needed for taking care of anything you might encounter during a snow storm. I always ate the candy bars in the survival kit before they went bad...and would replace the missing candy bars in the box from time to time. Someone had to do it! The tools, that was another story. I might have jumper cables in the car...but for me to jump anything would have probably ended in a total disaster. Some people are just dangerous with tools. You know it is a God thing when I tell you...during the whole 20 years I lived in Minnesota I only had two flats...both times, someone came along and fixed them for me. I have lived in Missouri for 3 years and have had 5 flats...two in one week. God just looked after me in special ways when I lived in Minnesota. I had the tools, but no knowledge of what to do with them. An emergency was an emergency for me!..stranded without the ability to care for myself. I was helpless in the case of an emergency.

Psalm 86

Bend down, O LORD, and hear my prayer; answer me, for I need your help. Protect me, for I am devoted to you. Save me, for I serve you and trust you. You are my God. Be merciful, O Lord, for I am calling on you constantly. Give me happiness, O Lord, for my life depends on you. O Lord, you are so good, so ready to forgive, so full of unfailing love for all who ask your aid. Listen closely to my prayer, O LORD; hear my urgent cry. I will call to you whenever trouble strikes, and you will answer me.

Nowhere among the pagan gods is there a god like you, O Lord. There are no other miracles like yours. All the nations—and you made each one—will come and bow before you, Lord; they will praise your great and holy name. For you are great and perform great miracles. You alone are God.

Teach me your ways, O LORD, that I may live according to your truth! Grant me purity of heart, that I may honor you. With all my heart I will praise you, O Lord, my God. I will give glory to your name forever, for your love for me is very great. You have rescued me from the depths of death.

O God, insolent people rise up against me; violent people are trying to kill me. And you mean nothing to them. But you, O Lord, are a merciful and gracious God, slow to get angry, full of unfailing love and truth. Look down and have mercy on me. Give strength to your servant; yes, save me, for I am your servant. Send me a sign of your favor. Then those who hate me will be put to shame, for you, O LORD, help and comfort me.

THIS IS A PICTURE OF A PERSON WHO IS IN TROUBLE...

I am not sure if his car broke down...or his chariot! We don't exactly know what brought him to this place. I do know his enemies were in hot pursuit of his life and had plans to kill him. Pretty serious trouble...he was needy and he was desperate. Have you been there? I have.

When an emergency comes into your life...what do you do?

What has happened in your life that has brought you to the end of yourself and you are finally forced to call out to God for help. In this case, David is being chased in hot pursuit by his enemies. They wanted his life and they were planning to kill him. This is a serious problem...and I don't think he was in Houston...he was needy and he was desperate. We have all been there!

David's request for the Lord to bend down and hear his prayer...totally disarms me. I cannot begin to think in these terms. The Lord God of heaven...bending down to hear my troubles...is this not where we must start with our helplessness and brokenness? Our lostness is so apparent without Him. It does not matter where you have been, what you have done...or the amount of sin which has plagued your life for years. You know, those besetting sins...God, wants you to be reconciled to Him through what His son has done on the cross for your sins and mine. We can come to Him...and He bends down...He actually came down from heaven. "He sent his only begotten son to the cross to die for our sins, all of our sins, in order that the justice of God might be satisfied."

Feelings of aloneness...and brokenness...is often where we have to be before we will turn our lives over to the Lord. My children...my family...we have been so lost...so desperate and God has met us every time. He has come to the rescue...over and over again.

"O Lord, you are so good, so ready to forgive, so full of unfailing love for all who ask your aid."

We have to come to the end of ourselves and our resources. → → → → → → → → → → → → → → →

"You alone are God." We have no other place to go...we have no one who can help us. If your life has been consumed by alcohol...pleasures...addictions...mental and emotional break-downs, divorce, prison, whatever...God is the only one, He alone can totally repair the damage caused by sin.

Kevin, a young man...who had to come to the end of himself...in a prison, was forced to face the fact that God alone, and ONLY God alone, could bail him out of the prison of disbelief. He was indeed hopeless and without any hope of being different. He was not in charge, he needed to be saved from his own self-destructive ways.

His anger, feelings of shame and blame, arrogance, all had taken him down a road of no return. The deceiver had lied to him about the reality of life and his choices were robbing him of any life, much less a life of abundance. A survivor of adoption, issues of abandonment, his parent's divorce, his own feelings of guilt over his own children and not being there for them... his thinking that the lies he had learned from the survivors of the streets were true had finally caught up with him and he found himself in a place where he could not run, he could not hide. He needed to know the truth, could the Jesus his mother talked to him about...be real? He wondered, if it was true would the God his mother trusted be willing to come to his aid. Would that God be someone he personally could trust?

His life was at the bottom of the heap. He had to make the decision to call out and ask God for help...

Teach me your ways, O LORD, that I may live according to your truth! Grant me purity of heart that I may honor you.

With all my heart I will praise you, O Lord my God. I will give glory to your name forever, for your love for me is very great. You have rescued me from the depths of death!

These verses...apply to Kevin's life and to many of us who have strayed from the truth and gone beyond the safety of the path. We have gone our own way...and found trouble to be in our face. Sin has walked with us and almost destroyed us...but God..and only God, can truly come to the rescue and heal whatever is broken.

Another young man...brought up knowing God but plagued by the sin of pornography. A slave to his own addiction, molested as a child... found himself in the midst of a serious emergency... his wife, finally saying, "this is it, we're not doing this anymore until you deal with your problem." Stopped along side of the road and broken down...needing the tools for freedom and a new lifestyle...needing desperately to make changes but gasping for breath and going down and under... over and over again. Desperately needing to be freed from the addiction, he was mastered by his sin...no freedom...only a slave to sin...because he believed the lies of the enemy. Hoping against all hope to break the chain of sin...and then finally finding victory.

Who in their right mind would choose to become a slave, caught up in sin to the point where your life is not your own. Yet addictions are taking people down paths of destruction daily. Substance abuse, workaholics, control freaks, anything that masters people. An addiction is relinquishing ourselves to the control of something or someone else. Submission to the will of God is the alternative choice. It is as though we are standing at the crossroads again, we have to make that choice...take that risk.

Romans 6:16

Don't you realize that whatever you choose to obey becomes your master? You can choose sin, which leads to death, or you can choose to obey God and receive his approval.

2 Peter 2:19

(These false teachers) promise freedom, but they themselves are slaves to sin and corruption. For you are a slave to whatever controls you.

Ephesians 5:15-20

So be careful how you live, not as fools but as those who are wise. Make the most of every opportunity for doing good in these evil days. Don't act thoughtlessly, but try to understand what the Lord wants you to do. Don't be drunk with wine, because that will ruin your life. Instead, let the Holy Spirit fill and control you. Then you will sing psalms and hymns and spiritual songs among yourselves, making music to the Lord in your hearts. And you will always give thanks for everything to God the Father in the name of our Lord Jesus Christ.

Romans 8:6

If your sinful nature controls your mind, there is death. But if the Holy Spirit controls your mind, there is life and peace.

The Tools are Available.

It is not that we aren't aware of our emergencies...we are... but we need to get out the tools and if we cannot repair it ourselves, we need to ask for help.

Galatians 6:1-3

Dear friends, if a Christian is overcome by some sin, you who are godly should gently and humbly help that person back onto the right path. And be careful not to fall into the same temptation yourself. Share each other's troubles and problems and in this way obey the law of Christ. If you think you are too important to help someone in need, you are only fooling yourself. You are really a nobody.

The Christian community thinks that being a spiritual person is entirely different from what God says a spiritual person is...a Spiritual or Godly person...is someone who comes along side of others caught in sin and helps pull them out of the ditch. He comes along and gets out his chain and hooks up his car to the other person's car in the ditch and pulls them out. He knows how to do this because he has been there himself...and he now carries his chain around with him ready at all times to stop along the road and give the other person a helping hand.

Many churches today are developing Care Giving Ministries... this is what Care Giving Ministries is really about. Coming along side of others who are in need of helpful, kind assistance. The best suited people for these ministries are those who have been through the emergencies. They have learned by surviving and living their own path what destruction sin can bring into a person's life because they have personally been affected by it.

In our church, we have such a ministry. People going through divorce can receive help from those who have experienced the pain of divorce. They know how to come along and give encouragement and help. God hates divorce...but it is not the unpardonable sin...and Christians are living through divorce.

Others had lived through abusive marriages and needed someone to come along side of them through the difficult time of getting out of the situation and into a place of safety. The Christian body pulling each other out of the ditch...how Biblical and how consistent with God's plan for us in learning to assist and care for one another. The body of Christ needs God and we need each other. We are not Islands.

We aren't all skilled to do the repair work...we may be just the one who comes along and pulls them out of the ditch and directs them to the professional help they really need. We stand by to offer them a ride home and conversation and assurance that everything will work out. This is why we need strong spiritual lay people to minister to one another. We need to be caring and non-judgmental in our ministry of helping people out of the ditch.

Emergencies may Force us to Face New Challenges...

People are not going to jump up and down and yell out to you or anyone along the road, "I need help!" It may take them time to trust you. Sometimes this happens as they are getting to know you. They are watching your life to see if they can trust you with the information about themselves and they are watching to see who you turn to when you are having a difficult time. Who do you turn to when you have an emergency? Do you know the number to dial for, "Road Service?"

It may be they have hidden their needs so well you would hardly recognize them as having an emergency. The depth of depression and mental illness today in the body of Christ is beyond belief. We are dealing with an epidemic of people suffering from mental illnesses. We are not equipped to come along side and help...but we can give support and we can encourage people to please get professional help.

Families are at risk because of mental illness. It must be dealt with in a healthy way. The scourge of mental illness is a plight that is causing the church to be weakened. We can stand against it. We can get help for our brothers and sisters in Christ. We can help to take away the shame and blame and choose to break down the barriers so others can be free or at least supported in their time of need. We can no longer hide the truth from others or ourselves. Our churches are full of hurting broken people who are struggling with not being able to think clearly, they cannot grow in their walk with the Lord until they are given some freedom from the mental anguish they are experiencing.

Proverbs 18:14

The human spirit can endure a sick body, but who can bear it if the spirit is crushed?

Children coming from broken homes who only can attend every other weekend need to be included and loved in special ways...reach out and risk. Teens who have become pregnant need support and love. Parents in pain because of children who have left the nest to be out there in the world...are bleeding and in need of our Care Givers Ministries. What can we do? How can we help? I am not totally certain...but we have to start somewhere...the cars are strewn along the road and the pile-ups are slowing down the traffic...and the tools are available, we just need to find someone who knows how to use them and then teach others to use them as well.

Many casualties are noted...but what are we doing to assist in the recovery of these dear friends. I pray we may be challenged to develop a training program for our churches. Ask God to give you courage to assist those who have been in the battle and have lost the first round. The ministry of reconciliation is what we need to be about in the Twenty First Century...not the concept in thinking, we aren't our brother's keepers.

We need to give hope and encouragement. The tools are available, we just need to make sure we have them in our survival kit. If we aren't able to use them, then we need to ask God for boldness to ask for help.

WORTHY EVENTS TO REMEMBER ALONG THE WAY...

1. Maybe you have been in an emergency...how did you feel? How did you manage to find a way out of the situation? Will you share your personal situation with others?

2 You who are Spiritual...and Godly...need to come along side of others. Use your past and allow God to recycle it... to turn it into good. The devil meant it for evil...but God meant it for good.

3 Do you have a Care Givers Ministry in your Church? Maybe you need to start one...or get involved with the present ministry already in place. Ask God to give you a compassionate heart.

4 Find out what tools you need...and ask someone to show you how to use them for the glory of the Lord.

5 Pray for your friends...those in your family first, then in your church...and in your neighborhoods...people who are broken down...and in need of God's truth. The truth and tools need to be shared with those who need assistance. Do it gently and with respect.

When we asked for bread, He didn't give us a stone; When we sought His presence, He didn't leave us alone; When we needed a Savior, He came from above; When our hearts were empty, He filled them with love.

In the time of our deepest need...God will be all we need! We need to share the truth ourselves and teach others to do the same.

Chapter Seven

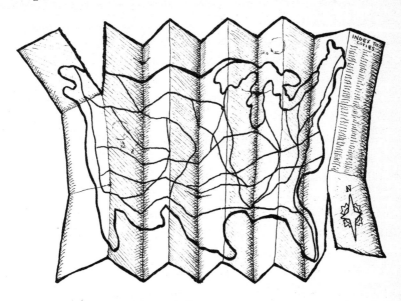

WE'RE ON THE ROAD...

WITH A PURPOSE AND A PLAN!

This idea of having a purpose and a plan is so difficult for me. I am a Recovering Messy...for crying out loud! This is not easy for me. Recovering from my messy ways, meant I had to make a huge change. I had to know what I was changing from so I could change to God's plan and not my own set of ideas. It didn't make sense in the beginning...but I knew I had to follow God's road...and His path...and I needed to stay in the car.

The Compass, The Focus. → → → → → → → → → →

I am in the car...my tank is full...heading for my destination. I started seeing all of these alternative routes as I was in the midst of my journey. I had a tremendous battle going on inside, which way do I go...and which direction do I take? Have you noticed how difficult it can be in the middle of the night trying to read the road signs? Just about the time, I come to a sign which gives me a little more direction...a huge truck gets in the way and blocks out my view. I continue to go down the road but clearly I have missed my turn-off. This happened to us as we were coming down from Minnesota to visit our children in St. Louis. Mom kept handing me change, we ended up paying all kinds of toll money because we missed the turn-off. I hate it when that happens!

Achieving our goals and realizing the fulfillment of our dreams and plans doesn't always happen overnight. We didn't after all, fall into our situation overnight and we aren't necessarily going to get out of the mess and on to the right road overnight. God has His own sense of timing and He does what He wants within His time frame. God requires for us to "walk by faith and not by sight," it can mean we will be taking several alternate routes. We can still be in the will of God even when God's plan and purpose seems confusing to us. I have had this experience personally several times.

God is not the author of confusion but I have been on the alternate route wondering around but still headed in the right direction. It feels like we are so out of control. Issues of control plague the Christian community and the secular world as well. Control issues are a definite distraction in finding God along the way.

We all want to know God's plan and have God spell it out for us...and "walking by faith and not by sight," will require total dependence upon the Lord and not upon ourselves.

We can ponder and plan but God is the One who knows the direction we need to go. He has the only road map and it is required reading if we are to finally achieve our final destination.

We can even try to help others avoid the pitfalls and potholes that we see in the road. We can plead with them, but we can only point them in the right direction. We cannot force them to come with us or make healthier choices. I can barely take responsibility for my own choices. I must first obey what God is calling me to do and then model it, or live it, and then encourage others to come along.

Collision Course...Without the Lord!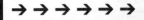

Ezekiel 3:20-21

If good people turn bad and don't listen to my warning, they will die. If you did not warn them of the consequences, then they will die in their sins. Their previous good deeds won't help them, and I will hold you responsible, demanding your blood for theirs. But if you warn them and they repent, they will live, and you will have saved your own life too.

I think it is important to warn people of destruction ahead. We are to clearly mark the signs but we cannot force people to accept Christ. It is the work of the Holy Spirit. He sends conviction into the lives of our friends and loved ones. On the other hand, we are to clearly warn others and give clear instructions as they are willing to hear. God, the Holy Spirit...is the One who brings conviction to the souls and hearts of men and women, boys and girls.

> *There had been a terrible flood and the waters had washed out the bridge up ahead...people discovered the destruction and had gotten out in the middle of the road. With waving lanterns, they tried to warn people to stop and to slow down. For some reason, some didn't slow down and the scary dark winding road was ahead... without a bridge. Some were able to determine the situation and stop...others were not and it was disastrous for their journey. How foolish we might say, and such a waste...how could they make that poor choice and jeopardize their lives and those passengers in their cars? Whatever the reason, they did not heed the warning.*

While we are not responsible for the actions and choices of

others, we are still to warn them of the consequences of sin. We are to tell them...because we do not want them to have to pay the toll or miss the bridge.

1 Peter 3:13-18

Now, who will want to harm you if you are eager to do good? But even if you suffer for doing what is right, God will reward you for it. So don't be afraid and don't worry. Instead, you must worship Christ as Lord of your life. And if you are asked about your Christian hope, always be ready to explain it. But you must do this in a gentle and respectful way. Keep your conscience clear. Then if people speak evil against you, they will be ashamed when they see what a good life you live because you belong to Christ. Remember, it is better to suffer for doing good, if that is what God wants, than to suffer for doing wrong!

Christ also suffered when he died for our sins once for all time. He never sinned, but he died for sinners **that he might bring us safely home to God**. He suffered physical death, but he was raised to life in the spirit.

Romans 3:23-26

For all have sinned; all fall short of God's glorious standard. Yet now God in his gracious kindness declares us not guilty. He has done this through Christ Jesus, who has freed us by taking away our sins. For God sent Jesus to take the punishment for our sins and to satisfy God's anger against us. We are made right with God when we believe that Jesus shed his blood, sacrificing his life for us. God was being entirely fair and just when he did not punish those who sinned in former times. And he is entirely fair and just in this present time when he declares sinners to be right in his sight because they believe in Jesus.

God wants to bring us **safely home**. He wants us to find our way and he clearly marks the path so we will not be confused by the alternative routes. He will give us clear direction, as we seek His plan for our lives...and His purpose for our lives. His Plan and His Purpose go hand in hand. God knows all of those who will come to Him and He will see that we have the opportunity to receive the message of hope and eternal life.

Living for God. → → → → → → → → → → → → →

It is a privilege to live for Christ...but it is also challenging. The ways of our old nature are so ingrained in us, we are often torn by the turmoil going on inside of us. It is a Spiritual battle. The old nature and the struggle of the new nature. It takes time and being in the word of God before we are able to make sound choices then live out our lives based upon those choices. This time frame can be very individualized...we are not little robots...we are cared for by a God who knows us each one in a personal way.

I have taken the old way home so often I just go my normal route...but then a new road was completed and I was forced to take the new road...it caused me to think about my exit and which was the right exit. I have driven past my exit several times, because I was not paying attention. It takes time and thought to live for Christ. I have to determine in my heart to follow the Lord in obedience. The old ways sometimes need to change.

Galatians 5:16-25

So I advise you to live according to your new life in the Holy Spirit. Then you won't be doing what your sinful nature craves. The old sinful nature loves to do evil, which is just opposite from what the Holy Spirit wants. And the Spirit gives us desires that are opposite from what the sinful nature desires. These two forces are constantly fighting each other, and your choices are never free from this conflict. But when you are directed by the Holy Spirit, you are no longer subject to the law.

When you follow the desires of your sinful nature, your lives will produce these evil results: sexual immorality, impure thoughts, eagerness for lustful pleasure, idolatry, participation in demonic activities, hostility, quarreling, jealousy, outbursts of anger, selfish ambition, divisions, the feeling that everyone is wrong except those in your own little group, envy, drunkenness, wild parties, and other kinds of sin. Let me tell you again, as I have before, that anyone living that sort of life will not inherit the Kingdom of God.

But when the Holy Spirit controls our lives, he will produce this kind of fruit in us: love, joy, peace, patience, kindness, goodness, faithfulness, gentleness, and self-control. Here, there is no conflict with the law.

Those who belong to Christ Jesus have nailed the passions and desires of their sinful nature to his cross and crucified them there. If we are living now by the Holy Spirit, let us follow the Holy Spirit's leading in every part of our lives.

Living for Christ is a challenge...and making a long trip is not easy. We have to make good preparations, and plans. We have to be willing to **STOP, LOOK, and LISTEN.** The simple message we learned from kindergarten is important for us as mature growing adults who desire to walk in the Spirit as we are called to live out our lives in obedience. It is the discipline that brings happiness and a sense of well-being as we complete the course and determine we will not get off on any side road. We are in the midst of a great journey. God has called us to the best.

Once we are in the car...we experience His peace. We are ready for the journey, we have our map and we have our survival kit. We are complete in Him.

Picking up hitchhikers.

One of the most exciting times in my life is when I am able to come along side of New Believers! They bless and encourage me. I have this sweet young couple in my life...Aaron and Ingrid, they have recently come to know the Lord. They signed up for a New Believers Bible Study, along with some others and we are studying the Roadmap together around the kitchen table. I am watching this small group grow in Christ right before my eyes. We are praying together...we are praying for each other, for their children and for their world. This part of the journey is the best! I love all of them. Dawn, Rich, Joy and Kevin...we are going forward in our faith... and we are learning about following the road signs for clear instructions.

Are you investing your time with others on a daily basis? It may be your family, your children, your neighbors. Are you spending time with New Believers and taking time to explain to them the importance of "being on the road." How will they know about the pitfalls and potholes if you are not sharing with them what you have learned and how to avoid those painful distractions. We are sitting in the car...and we have been over the road many times. We know the way...and we know where to find the truth in God's word. We are the tourist guide specialists!

When we are picking up hitchhikers...they need to be assured of a safe environment as they are learning. We must ask them to join us as we are busy going down the road. They need to be treated with respect and concern as we consider how we can assist them along their way as they are seeking helpful information to assist them in finding the goal of their destination.

We are all on the road together after all, and at some point someone needed to help us and give us direction. We tend to forget this part of the journey. We forget how God placed people in our lives to help us. This part of sharing our lives with others will give us a healthy perspective of serving and demonstrating love in a real sense of the word.

Galatians 5:13

For you, dear friends, have been called to live in freedom—not freedom to satisfy your sinful nature, but freedom to serve one another in love.

Galatians 6:1

Dear friends, if a Christian is overcome by some sin, you who are godly should gently and humbly help that person back onto the right path. And be careful not to fall into the same temptation yourself.

Our hitchhikers can be fellow Christians who have lost their way and need a helping hand along the way. Making room in our cars for others and providing guidance is a great gift of love and it will also remind us of where we have been and where we are going.

Never forget your own path. Understanding God's ways is key, we must see beyond the moment to the final work that He is doing in and through us. We must never judge the circumstances or situation prematurely. God is not finished with any of us yet. We are a work or a road in progress. There is more to be seen and known. We never stop learning about the path.

Having a clear understanding of our focus is so important. I cannot stress this concept enough. Serving ourselves only robs us of the joy of serving the Lord and others. The focus of self... has been a hot topic since the 70's. We have been warned over and over again about the dangers of focusing only upon ourselves. We need to focus our entire lives upon the fact that we are called to be servants. It is a high calling. When this calling is confused, it can destroy any good work we might be called to do as servants of the King.

Self indulgence shows itself in various ways:

⬡ **WE HAVE TO BE IN CONTROL...**

⬡ **CO-DEPENDENCY ISSUES...**

⬡ **NO LEGITIMATE BOUNDARIES AND DISCIPLINE...**

⬡ **WE BECOME OUR OWN IDOL...**

We are not pallet people but pedestal people.

When we are Self Focused, we Cannot Pick Up hitchhikers!

We begin asking the wrong questions. Who will notice what I have done, and who will get the glory for this gracious act of kindness? Look at all the time it has taken to pick someone else up and put them into my car along with their baggage... and don't forget the baggage. It took a great sacrifice to pick up that poor needy person. Oh yes, how self righteous we become when we are not being a servant. It is a calling. I recall something like this in the Bible.

Luke 10:30-37

Jesus replied with an illustration:"A Jewish man was traveling on a trip from Jerusalem to Jericho, and he was attacked by bandits. They stripped him of his clothes and money, beat him up, and left him half dead beside the road.

"By chance a Jewish priest came along; but when he saw the man lying there, he crossed to the other side of the road and passed him by. A Temple assistant walked over and looked at him lying there, but he also passed by on the other side.

"Then a despised Samaritan came along and when he saw the man, he felt deep pity. Kneeling down beside him, the Samaritan soothed his wounds with medicine and bandaged them. Then he put the man on his own donkey and took him to an inn, where he took care of him. The next day he handed the innkeeper two pieces of silver and told him to take

care of the man. 'If his bill runs higher than that,' he said, 'I'll pay the difference the next time I am here.'

"Now which of these three would you say was a neighbor to the man who was attacked by bandits?" Jesus asked.

The man replied, "The one who showed him mercy." Then Jesus said, "Yes, now go and do the same."

Picking up hitchhikers may mean you have to invite them into your home for awhile...or you may have to take care of their kids for awhile...or you may have to prepare some meals for them, or help them with things they cannot do on their own. Those are the practical things we are called to do...not to mention the Spiritual care that is also validated by the practical gifts we have each been given for the express purpose of serving and giving care to others. Our gifts are given to us to benefit the body of Christ...and we are to be about building His Kingdom...one hitchhiker at a time.

How we view ourselves effects how we relate to God and others. We cannot allow our warped cultural concept of who we are to define who we are in Christ. Jesus is our example of serving and look who he picked up along the way...fishermen, tax collectors, common ordinary folks, trained and cared for by Jesus, taught to follow his example. Our thinking and feeling process needs a Spiritual Reality Check based upon the word of God and what He says, we are called to be and do.

It is certainly a stretch for some of us when we are forced into meeting new people and coming along side of others. It takes us beyond and out of our comfort zone...but it is also about "becoming all things to all people in order to win some." We cannot afford the luxury of excusing ourselves because we are shy or into ourselves, we have to move beyond our own fears...and walk by faith not fear.

Moving out in faith and beyond our own little world is a Spiritual Challenge. It means being transparent; we have to get over the fear of letting others know us for real. It is important that we reach out to the lost people of our world...we must say, "yes, I can do that." It is often easier to write out a check, but sometimes God calls us to go out into the neighborhood and be visible...to be a testimony for the Lord and tell others about our new journey. If we had a brand new, still has the new car smell...car, you can believe...we would be showing it off...to anyone in the neighborhood that would listen. "How about coming along for a ride in my new car?" I'd love to be able to invite someone to do that with me...am I as anxious to invite others to some function at my Church? I have to also ask myself if I am eager to share my walk with the Lord? I pray so!

I believe one of the Psychological Diseases of our modern culture is the obsession of self. Our consumer society mass markets beauty, youth, and material success...we are constantly bombarded with images of people we view as better than ourselves... and we stop short of sharing the gospel message with others because we are not sure how **we will be received...rather than being concerned that others need to be picked up and helped along the way.** The tendency to compare ourselves with the perfect body, face, job, or intelligence can cause us to miss an opportunity because we feel inadequate. Jesus encourages us to locate the proper source of self- esteem. Our lives are of infinite worth, not because of who we are on our own...but who Christ says we are...we are his chosen people called to come along and pick up hitchhikers.

Ecclesiastes 11:4

If you wait for perfect conditions, you will never get anything done.

Bottom line...as the Car Racers often say, "We just go out there and do the very best we can!"

Have you ever found yourself going down the road and you come to a place where it is time to merge into another busy lane of traffic...while you wait, car after car passes you not slowing down even a little. Finally a magnanimous and kind person slows down and motions for you to come on in and join the flow of traffic. You give them a wave and honor them for their kindness.

Jesus reminds us that we honor him when we seek the best not for ourselves but for others.

Luke 14:12-14

Then he turned to his host. "When you put on a luncheon or a dinner," he said, "don't invite your friends, brothers, relatives, and rich neighbors. For they will repay you by inviting you back. Instead, invite the poor, the crippled, the lame, and the blind. Then at the resurrection of the godly, God will reward you for inviting those who could not repay you."

This is a great place to be in our Christian walk...able to give others a ride and a bit of encouragement along the way. It is about offering them a cool drink from the "water of life."

Luke 11:28

"But even more blessed are all who hear the word of God and put it into practice."

WORTHY EVENTS TO REMEMBER ALONG THE WAY...

1. Have you made the decision to follow Christ until you reach the heavenly home? If not, maybe you would like to ask Christ into your heart and life. You can do that by simply praying this simple prayer:

Father in heaven, I know that I have sinned against you and you alone. I have not lived my life in any way shape or form to please you as my creator. I confess my sins...all of them, and trust that because you said you would forgive me, you will. Come into my heart and life right now and help me to know that I am saved based upon what your Son did on the cross for me.

I thank you Jesus for dying for my sins. I believe that you rose from the grave because you have power over all things, and one day you will come again for those who have trusted in you for salvation. I accept your gift to me. Thank you and help me to get into the car and do my journey with you rather than trying to figure out my own way.

Amen.

2. Who picked you up along the way as you were going down the road? Have you picked up any hitchhikers along the way lately? Remember your path and who helped you along the way.

3. Do not allow your fears to keep you from loving others in a practical way. Start today thinking of others who may need a ride. Ask God to help you be real in the midst of those who are seeking a new path.

4. If you have been trying to find your own path and have gotten off the road onto an alternative path ask the Father to restore to you the joy of your salvation. Thank Him for His guidance and help along the way.

Maybe instead of filling in the potholes in your present road...you may need to ask God to help you build a whole new road.

Chapter Eight ▰▰▰

WE'RE ON THE ROAD...

"THE CAR NEEDS WHAT?"

I had been hearing these little weird sounds...like, chug, clunk, chug, chug, grind. I pulled into my favorite mechanics place of business...and asked, "Could you please listen to my car? I think something is wrong." Dave took it for a spin...and yes indeed, something was wrong. "A broken block...and how much did you say it was going to cost?" I called my son and he told me that was in the ball park for what I needed and did I have the money to get it fixed?

I Don't Do Well With Negative Information! → → → →

How do you handle negative information? Most of us think we can handle just about anything but not really...especially when it is going to involve an outlay of cash. We get a bit nervous and our trust level goes way down.

→ → → → → → → → → →

God had already provided for this need of a new block back in August. A man knocked at my door and asked me if I was aware of a Class Action against the people who had installed the Masonite on the outside of my house. He asked me if I knew I was entitled to a certain amount of money if I would fill out the necessary forms? "Well no, quite frankly, I didn't know." I did know my house needed painting. I even planned to do it in the Spring. I could see the black areas on the side of my house. The masonite looked unsightly, but I thought in my ignorance a good coat of paint will do the trick...Wrong!

But now God was going to provide some money for me. I thought, isn't this a neat thing from the Lord...and what would I really be needing the money for after all was said and done. It all comes around...and in December my car needed a new block. I am still not certain what a new block really means, but I did know the sounds my car was making, chug, clunk, chug, grind. When you hear these sounds, you need to know it is going to cost money...and be sure of this, you had better know a good mechanic—one you can trust. God had provided for me in August for the coming December. He has a plan and a purpose for our lives. I keep saying this to myself because it is incredible to me how He does provide for all of our needs.

Philippians 4:6

Don't worry about anything; instead, pray about everything.

I had prayed about my car many times, you have to pray when you have that many miles on an old car. I prayed God would be faithful and supply my needs and take care of me as I travel around getting lost. He does care for me, it is so automatic His care for me...that I often take it for granted.

1 Peter 5:7 (paraphrased)

Cast all of your cares upon Him, for he cares about you.

Cast your **car upon Him...for He cares for your car!** I love how God looks after us.

How do You Handle Negative News About Others?

I don't like hearing bad things about others. I hate to hear when those I love are sick, worried, or stressed out. I can sometimes sense when things are not good for my family in Mesa. Many times I just call them and say, "What is Happening?" I know something isn't right and the Lord has laid them upon my heart and I just start to pray. I usually have to call because I need to know how they are and how I can better pray for them.

I had some concerns for Dan and his family for a number of months. I was concerned about their lack of Spiritual Growth... Mothers have concerns.

One evening in December, I received a call in the middle of the night. "Mom, please pray, just pray...Oh Mom it is terrible"...and the phone went dead. I could not tell if it was Dan or Tim...their voices are both so alike it could have been either one of them calling me on a cell phone. Mike didn't have a cell phone at that time. I fell to the floor and started to pray for both of them. I didn't know if Tim was at work and a plane had crashed, or he was in some serious accident. I didn't know where Dan was at this time of the night or what could be happening in his life. I just prayed for them...I called out to God, please, God help my sons!

A few minutes later the phone rang again, I could tell this time it was Dan...I was more awake. He started to tell me about his friend Rob...and how he and his Dad had been in a very, very, serious plane crash, and Dan...said, "Mom, I could have been on that plane, I was going to be on that plane." It was a serious plane crash and Dan watched helplessly. He was waiting for them to land along with his friend John... and the plane hit a telephone pole and missed the runway. His friend was burned over 45% of his body. Rob's Dad died as a result of his injuries.

Dan was calling again from the cell phone and headed to the hospital in Tucson. He was asking me to pray...for me to pray for his friend...he was in a serious unstable condition. It was touch and go. Dede, (Dan's wife) and Chris, (a friend) were headed to the hospital driving from Phoenix. Dede had called too asking for prayer. It was all so scary.

Dan told me about his friend Rob, who along with his Dad, called by his friends, "Doc" were flying up to help him with his business meeting. "Doc", was the pilot and also an instructor. Dan had hoped to take lessons in the future from "Doc." They were flying up for a meeting to help my son with their mutual business interests.

His Dad had flown into this little airport many times. It was familiar and even though it was at night, he knew the lay of the land. The airstrip had a slope going up for landing and going down for taking off...the lights on the airstrip were not turned on. Dan's friend drove to the end of the airstrip and turned on the lights of their truck believing it would make a difference. "Doc", the pilot had circled several times and then decided to come in for a landing...but somehow came in short of the runway...hitting a telephone pole...the plane crashed and went up in flames. No one doubted his abilities to land the plane. It was an accident that changed so many lives. It changed my son's life forever.

Dan ran as fast as he could to the sight of the crash...falling, and running, trying to get to the scene of the accident. Several people had gathered...Rob doesn't know exactly how they got out of the plane unless he and his Dad had been carried out by angels...who knows! So many things to think about and ponder.

It happened so quickly, my son could hardly believe his eyes. Rob and his Dad experienced life and death in a matter of seconds. No one could have predicted this tragedy.

Months later, sitting around in the livingroom at Rob's home, talking about the accident reminded us that we might never know all that occurred on that night just a few months ago. God was there. We all understood His presence through this difficult time.

Dan's friend was coming to help him...flying in to give him encouragement in their business. God was bringing help to Dan in a different way than Dan had expected. God was sending Rob to help Dan in a way he could never have imagined. Dan needed to be Spiritually connected to God again.

God had sent a special servant in the midst of a horrible accident to bring Dan back into a vital and living relationship with Himself!

Dan and Dede and Christopher...rescued...Oh God how Awesome and Loving You are...in the midst of negative and horrible news, You reign!

When Dan's Dad was taken home, it left a huge black hole inside of Dan's heart and nothing seemed able to heal it. Dan lost confidence in God and his character as a faithful, loving and caring God. Dan had been at the hospital when his Dad went home and he couldn't understand why God had taken his Dad home. It was a loss he hadn't been able to deal with all of this time. His father's death didn't make sense and he couldn't plug up the anger or release it either. It had dulled all of his senses and caused him pain beyond belief.

Rob was now in the same position Dan had been in a few years earlier. Dan was running between Rob and his Dad...telling each about the other. It would be days before Rob would actually be told of his father's home-going. Rob was severely burned and living with pain and confusion...he was facing weeks and months of surgeries and skin grafting. We prayed that he would not lose his fingers or his toes...we prayed for his eye and his sight.

Dan watched and visited during this time being faced with his own painful memories and the loss of his Dad. Again, being forced and confronted with the question, he had asked himself so many times over the past few years, "God why do you allow these kinds of things to happen to good people?"

Dan's anger and feelings took him down a path away from the church, away from the place where he could have found encouragement and comfort. The Church only reminded him of his Dad's preaching and his strong tenor voice singing those hymns of praise...it was painful to hear the music he had grown up with and loved his whole life. Those memories haunted Dan and still Dan was silent, stuffing his emotions. God had not moved. He was still in Dan's life working his will and his way in gentle kind ways, and now this tragic accident happened right before his eyes. Dan had isolated himself from God hoping perhaps the pain would go away and somehow the loss of his Dad would not be a reality.

Now Dan was calling upon God for help...help for his friend and their family. It was during this time that God and Dan reconnected...as he prayed over the weeks for Rob, his friend...Dan was being drawn into the presence of the Lord in such a powerful way. Rob's pastor became a friend to Dan and came along side of their whole family. Stephanie, Rob's wife was clinging to the Lord for her strength to just be there at the hospital. Her witness was strong and Rob's Mom Fran was a witness to Dan. He was reminded again of God's faithfulness to His children.

Dan could see they were trusting in God. God was healing Rob's body. Rob was finally told of his Dad's fate...and he suffered the loss of not being aware of his Dad's home-going. Dan and Rob were experiencing the loss of their fathers... Christian Godly men who had loved and cared for them over many years...now they are in heaven. Rob and Dan had to deal with the loss in a conscious awareness of God. God being there but allowing His will to be made perfect in Bill's and Doc's lives.

The children of Rob Terrell were also brought into this circle of growth and blessing and pain. They had trusted God for their Dad...they had prayed and given an offering asking God to bring their Dad home from the hospital in 58 days. A letter from their pastor gives you an idea of how this event has come home to the children.

February 12, 2001

Dear Chelsea, Nathan, Alayna, and David:

A few weeks ago the church received your special faith offering. When I opened it, I wasn't sure how to respond; in the 17 years I have been in ministry, I have never been involved in such a gift. At first it touched me emotionally; this whole "adventure" that your dad is going through is emotionally difficult for all of us...and especially for you! I had to step away from my desk and take a minute to compose myself.

After a few days, I thought a lot about what your offering meant. We know that we cannot pay God to do things for us. However, there are many times in the Bible that people brought offerings of things that were valuable to them in response to promises that God made to them. That is what I think you did; you gave an offering to God because He made a promise to you to heal your dad. I believe God will honor your act of faith and do all that He has promised to you... and even more than you could imagine!

Your church family is looking forward to seeing all of you again very soon. We are praying for you daily. We believe that God is proving His love to each of you every day and this hard time will be used by Him to make you into the men and women of God that He can use for His plans.

We love you very much! Thank you for helping me grow in my faith by demonstrating your faith in such a meaningful way!

Growing in faith with you,

Pastor Bruce

Rob did come home from the hospital within that time frame as a Praise and Testimony to the faithfulness of God to his children. Others in the church where Dan and Rob attend experienced encouragement and blessings, too. Others from their mutual business also experienced God in a real way. So many were being touched by God's will in their lives.

February 13, 2001

Dear Rob,

I was attending the Sunday morning service at Winter Conference when Don called you on the cell phone. What you said had a profound affect on me.

I was raised with a great deal of religion that was fear based and oppressive to women. Because of that I turned to a belief system based around astrology and tarot cards. In fact I was a licensed astrologer for several years. I have always believed there is a God, but never quite trusted him. My faith was in the ability to predict my future and therefore control it. However this belief system began to fail me recently and I was struggling with where to turn. The more my astrology and tarot cards failed the harder I grasped and clung to such a belief. Until Sunday morning.

When you shared with us your dream about the yellow scarf, I saw the room we were in literally light up and I felt a gentle breeze swirl around me and fill my lungs at the same time I struggled to breathe. I closed my eyes against the tears that filled my eyes and saw a yellow scarf.

When I got home I knew without a shadow of a doubt what I had to do. I got rid of all of my astrology books, tarot cards, software and files. I was able to release 15 years of struggle and fear and I turned toward God. I bought my first bible and now I read it every day and pray each night, thanking God for the blessings he has brought me.

Since then I have experienced many miracles and have been shown that I am on the right path.

There is no doubt in my mind that without this business I wouldn't have had the opportunity to change my beliefs, because it was you sharing your heart and story that was the catalyst to my change. Although we have never actually met (I've taken many of your seminars and listened to many of your tapes) you are the gift from God that I needed and brought light into my life.

Thank you for your courage and strength to be the inspiration that you are for so many.

Blessing to you and your family,

Wendy Chandler

My children were in another one of God's Creative Crisis!

"The devil meant it for evil but God meant it for good." Dan and Dede and Christopher back in church. The safe place.

The doctors and nurses watched the healing process. Rob was supposed to be in the hospital for months, but his actual stay was shorter. His healing process is just that...it isn't over for him...and he is dealing with places on his body that need to heal and be restored. God is able! Rob's physical pain reminds him constantly that he must rely upon God every day of the healing process.

A few weeks ago, a friendly caring guy moved into the seat next to Dan in church. This young man, father of four...courageous and brave...sitting with my son in Church. They are in a safe place, sitting together seeking healing and hope from God in the midst of their losses.

John 16:33

...Here on earth you will have many trials and sorrows. But take heart, because I have overcome the world.

Matthew 5:4

"God blesses those who mourn, but they will be comforted."

2 Thessalonians 2:16-17

May our Lord Jesus Christ...who...gave us everlasting comfort and good hope, comfort your hearts and give you strength in every good thing you do and say.

We need to know that our words and our thoughts often take us places we do not want to go. We feel overwhelmed. When Dave my mechanic, told me my car needed some major work...I momentarily forgot that God had already provided for my need long before I needed the car to be repaired. The money came in the mail...the week I needed it...not before, just when I needed it. I had been praying and so had Mike and Tim and their families for Dan and his grief process. God used

109

a terrible thing to bring him to his knees. I believe that Dan knew his life could have been taken in the crash...but God had given him the gift of life. **No one knows the hour or the time...our days are numbered and in the hand of God...who knows all things.**

The wonderful group of friends Dan and Rob have in their business are there for them. They really do care and support one another. The people in the Church have cared and supported the Terrell's in such a loving way. God uses negative things in the midst of our ordinary lives to remind us of His concern and love for us. God is about using people in the real world of business and everyday living. We are responsible to share the gospel with others as we meet them in the marketplace, in our neighborhoods and along the way.

2 Corinthians 1:3-4

All praise to the God and Father of our Lord Jesus Christ. He is the source of every mercy and the God who comforts us. He comforts us in all our troubles so that we can comfort others. When others are troubled, we will be able to give them the same comfort God has given us.

The comforted becomes the comforter. That is the role God has for us. As He comforts us in our time of trouble so we will be able to comfort others.

Growing through Negative Situations.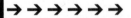

Romans 8:28

And we know that God causes everything to work together for the good of those who love God and are called according to his purpose for them.

Growth doesn't happen in our lives based upon our plan. God teaches us about Himself through simple mundane happenings...or through difficult and complex situations. I cannot predict God or what He will do next. I can barely figure out where to turn around when I find myself on a dead end street.

I admit, I need help...all the time. I need to be able to trust in someone bigger than myself. I am tired of trying to pull or put things together. I can't even change a tire...if the truth be known. I am not a mechanic, but I sure know how to drive down the road...I just pray it is not a one way street. I ask God daily to guide me and come along side of me and point me in the right direction.

My hope is built on nothing less...than Jesus blood and His Righteousness. I know enough to be dangerous at times.

I know I am in the car...and I do know that whatever is going on...I am safe...but when our lives seem to be headed down a one way street and our breaks aren't working, it is normal for me to believe a lie. We assume that God is off somewhere on a vacation leaving us to deal with the junk, but in truth, He is walking with us and caring for us. We may think we have lost our way...and it does feel sometimes like we are truly lost... but God made the road and He knows where each one of us is along the way.

Proverbs 4:23-27

Above all else, guard your heart, for it affects everything you do.

Avoid all perverse talk; stay far from corrupt speech.

Look straight ahead, and fix your eyes on what lies before you. Mark out a straight path for your feet; then stick to the path and stay safe. Don't get sidetracked; keep your feet from following evil.

I am grateful for God's provision along the way. I am glad for the signs...I do read them, unless a truck has gotten in the way. I do try and follow the directions of others, especially if I know they have been to the place where I am trying to go... Stop, Look, and Listen is such a healthy way to view the path.

God cares about our children and our families. He takes them where they need to be...He brings people into their lives for the express purpose of bringing them back to Himself.

We can trust Him as we travel around in the car.

WORTHY EVENTS TO REMEMBER ALONG THE WAY...

1. Why do we allow fear to rule our judgement...when we hear sounds that make us afraid...like chug, clunk, chug, grind?

2. Has the enemy taken you down a dead end street...and you are feeling hopeless? How can you get back on the path?

3. Losses are so devastating...we hide, we run, and we isolate...We need to help each other remember that it is a process. It takes time. Scars tell us that healing has taken place.

Some days, I think I am doing very well...and then something comes up. I feel very fragile and lost. A fragrance, a memory, a song and I am in the fog... like a patch of ground fog that moves in from nowhere surrounding me on my road...for a brief moment...I am in the thick of it and I am forced to slow down...and move with caution, I pray it will soon be lifted. Along with my broken spirit...I ask for healing to come into my heart and life. It is during those times when we are given the assurance that our Redeemer is near...and our anchor will hold.

4. God's grace is sufficient for all of our needs...in times of trials and testings...it is very difficult to count it all joy. Pray that you will allow Him to cover you today and renew your spirit and give you back your ability to walk in freedom from guilt. Loss and guilt destroy us. Loss with God gives us hope.

Our God the Healer!

Chapter Nine ▰▰▰▰

WE'RE ON THE ROAD...

WITH OUR LUNCH...AND STOPPING ALONG THE WAY!

I love picnics...and I love stopping along the way. We used to find the quaintest little out of the way spots, charming out-of-the-way places...I realized years later, why we found those places...they were cheap, and free. We found out that our fun time had to be cheap or free. We packed picnics and off we would go down to the ocean for hours of wonderful exciting entertainment, cost free. We have many memories and tubs of shells.

Plan to Laugh! → → → → → → → → → → → → → →

Did you know you can **Drive the Blues Away with Laughter?** Yes, you can, just don't drive too fast. Sometimes in the midst of our living situations our lives become stressful and high-maintenance. I tell people to take time out and do something fun. It is important lest we forget, there is healing in humor. I have watched people in airports and they can be pretty tense...waiting for people, flights delayed for whatever reason, missing their previous flights cause people to behave in various ways, some are ready to climb the walls. They are on their phones, on their computers and wrestling with kids, eating and drinking but it is obvious to me, few are laughing. Their faces tell it all...

Laughter is contagious in a good way. It is catching. People can pick up on people who are thinking in terms of the cup being empty or half full. The difference is our perspective. I love being with my family during our reunions...We do not have a perfect family by far...but we know how to laugh. Uncle Walter can spin a tale, told for the sole purpose of getting us all to laugh. His perspective is to view the world from the glass being half full. Walt and Janet lost their beautiful daughter to a killer disease and they have had to move forward and onward...finding much joy in their grandchildren and living life.

We can only really laugh when we feel we are in a safe environment. I have laughed so hard with my family that I started to cry. The emotion of laughter and crying feels very similar... and you have heard others talk about, "tears of joy," we need to release the pent-up emotions inside, down deep and have a good belly laugh. Children bring laughter to our hearts. They are themselves, funny and open. Little children bring laughter and hope to our feelings when we have been dealing with hurt, and being broken.

Where is the picnic when we are experiencing pain, betrayal, and loss of friendship? Our emotions are very close to the surface in times of pain. We also experience emotions coming from happy events, a new baby in the family, a wedding, a promotion...**or a new car!** We experience a flux of feelings when we are experiencing life. Pain and sorrow, joy and rewards, excitement prevails...and the emotion of laughter should be one that comes from deep within us, where we live.

Painful emotions often rob us of our joy. If we are living with unconfessed sin in our lives, the Holy Spirit has been quenched and our joy has flat-lined. Emotions that come from living in bondage make us sick.

Psalm 119:93

I will never forget your commandments, for you have used them to restore my joy and health.

Having the word of God solid in my heart and life restores to me my joy and my health. My spirit is restored and my heart rejoices. Our joy and our health go hand in hand. The promises of God play a huge part in the restoration of our thinking. Healing is such a needed commodity in our stress-filled lives. We are often forced to seek help when it becomes too much to bear.

Ephesians 4:20-24

But that isn't what you were taught when you learned about Christ. Since you have heard all about Him and have learned the truth that is in Jesus, throw off your old evil nature and your former way of life, which is rotten through and through, full of lust and deception. Instead, there must be a spiritual renewal of your thoughts and attitudes. You must display a new nature because you are a new person, created in God's likeness—righteous, holy, and true!

When Sarah, in the Old Testament, found out she was going to have a child...her laughter released the tension she had been holding on to for all of those years. Her shame was now going to be blotted out as she experienced the joy at ninety years old the inexpressible joy of bearing a son in her old age...the promised son from God to Abraham and Sarah. When the child was born she said:

Genesis 21:1-7 NIV

Now the Lord was gracious to Sarah as he had said, and the Lord did for Sarah what he had promised. Sarah became pregnant and bore to Abraham in his

old age, at the very time God had promised him.
Abraham gave him the name Isaac to the son Sarah
bore him. When his son Isaac was eight days old,
Abraham circumcised him as God commanded him.
Abraham was a hundred years old when his son
Isaac was born to him. Sarah said, "God has brought
me laughter, and everyone who hears about this will
laugh with me." And she added, "Who would have
said to Abraham that Sarah would nurse children?
Yet I have born him a son in his old age."

Laughter would be one way to handle this situation. I personally can't imagine it. Mom, who is ninety, and I, have talked about this event in God's word. Several times, when we have been out shopping or just tired from working in the garden our comment has been, *"thank God, we don't have a baby!"*

I realize that depression is a very real problem and people cannot just laugh and pretend the situation doesn't exist...but there is a prescription that professionals give, it is called Laughter Therapy...and it does encourage and help others in the midst of their depression. I have talked with people who have been dealing with loss and a chronic illness or depression, I always suggest first, they should seek professional help and Christian counseling...but I also mention to them to remember to get a good dose of Laughter along the way. It is helpful in the process of helping others deal with the problems of life.

Psalm 30:5b

Weeping may go on all night, but joy comes with the morning.

Psalm 30:11

You have turned my mourning into joyful dancing, You have taken away my clothes of mourning and clothed me with joy, that I might sing praises to you and not be silent. O LORD my God, I will give you thanks forever!

Stopping Along the Way...Means Taking Action.

If you plan to stop on the main highway, you will need to find an exit. Finding a rest stop along the way is a way of refreshing yourself as you are going down the road. Not everyone can drive and drive for hours without stopping. Little children and old ladies need frequent stops. Not everyone has a camel bladder!

A Acknowledge the pain....this is the first step in the healing process.

C Confess your anger and allow God to refresh your spirit. Be open to humor and healing.

T Take it one day at a time...each mile takes you closer to your destination of Hope.

I Invest your life in the lives of others. You will receive strength to do this work.

O Open your hand again, so you can receive Love and Laughter from the Lord.

N Never give up or give in. God forgives and restores.

The rest stop is often a time to change drivers. Share with others your burdens and allow them to share with you some of their burdens, learn how to come along side of one another. It makes the travel time less stressful and the passenger gets a chance to view the scenery. It is relaxing to just view the mountains or the ocean or life. We don't always have to participate to benefit from the ride. We can at times be the passengers or drivers...and even back-seat drivers or hitch-hikers. In the family car there is room.

Proverbs 17:22

A cheerful heart is a good medicine, but a broken spirit saps a person's strength.

Psalm 147:3 (paraphrased)

God promises to heal the broken hearted.

117

Malachi 4:2a

But for you who fear my name the Sun of Righteousness will rise with healing in his wings.

God will heal and restore us.

In Indian culture, we often laugh at ourselves. We tell things on ourselves and then we all laugh together. There is no shame when something happens to us, we are the first to expose ourselves and then it gives others permission to laugh with us. This develops into a great tale we will tell over and over again, squeezing out all the laughter we can from the experience. It is a good thing.

Plan a picnic...or a party...call up your friends and laugh together. I cannot tell a joke. I always forget the punch line or mess up the delivery of the joke...but I can tell you about life, and the stories from life are full of laughter more than dull jokes. My used-to-be boss, Paul Harkness...used to tell jokes and he would laugh the most...because they were jokes relating to Norwegians and he felt like he was telling tales on his family. My pastor loves to tell funny things...in the pulpit. He ends up laughing so hard, we join in with him and laugh... even if it isn't that funny. Laughter is contagious, it is good for us. The enemy would love to disrupt our journey and rob us of our joy.

There is Joy in the Journey.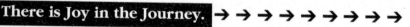

Zephaniah 3:17a

For the LORD your God has arrived to live among you. He is a mighty savior.

God will live among us with great joy.

I have been on some really rough roads. I have traveled to places I really didn't care to go. I can tell you I have not always experienced the "joy in the journey." I have participated but not with a sense of joy or excitement. I have kicked and screamed all along the way. I have learned one or two things along the path. If God is calling you to do something, do it. If

He is calling you to go someplace, you had better go. I would even suggest do it quickly. Don't put it off...the task or the opportunity is provided for you by the Lord himself and the longer you put it off the longer it takes to accomplish the purpose. There is no joy in running from God...ask Jonah!

Psalm 16:8-9

"I know the LORD is always with me...no wonder my heart is filled with joy..."

When we know the Lord's presence in our lives we will be able to rest and find contentment. I do not think wandering around and feeling lost gives us a sense of peace. There is no comfort for us if we choose to stay in our comfort zone. No parking, means No Parking!

I was forced to experience some rather discouraging side-trips along the way. The car breaking down, losing my way, there were times when there was no room in the Inn... and you couldn't even find an Inn...you had to sleep along side of the road or in a parking lot...but always knowing the Lord was with me, and I was in the car. I could be peaceful and His spirit was guiding me along the path. I have found times of joy in these times of stress...which amazes even me.

Faithfulness in a job well done, knowing we have done His will...gives a person a certain amount of joy. When I worked at KDNW in Duluth...there were times when I just felt like I had put in my time. It wasn't all that exciting. It was very hard work. I didn't always love doing the nitty gritty things especially if it didn't seem like ministry to me. Being faithful in the little things can be a chore if you aren't feeling called to do it, or you think you are above the opportunity. Work is boring and tedious for all of us at different times. Have you ever driven down a dull and boring stretch of highway? We have to be careful not to fall asleep, it takes effort and discipline to stay alert.

I used to dream up new methods for doing the routine tasks just to make them interesting and challenging. I had to redefine my calling and purpose many times. It wasn't about the job...it was about being faithful in the small things so God could do mighty things through the programming of the station, or it was about God blessing some small thing to bring honor and glory to His name.

I put a sign above the door of my office that said, "Well done, thou good and faithful servant." How silly is that! Mom always says, "Even a dog deserves a pat on the head." Sometimes, a sense for the journey is key...and finding joy in the midst of a dull boring journey is hard to come by. We may have to be creative, or remember the purpose, or check our attitude. Sometimes we have to remember why we are doing what we are doing.

James 2:26

Just as the body is dead without a spirit, so also faith is dead without good deeds.

Being human and sometimes wanting that pat on the head gets us thinking more about ourselves and our path, rather than having the focus be on Christ whom we serve. We simply lose sight of the final destination. God has to remind us that this life time is a journey...a job well done brings a deep sense of satisfaction and causes us to have joy in our hearts. We must remember the journey isn't over and the reward for service hasn't been settled yet.

I need to remind myself, the journey is not about me...but about whom I serve. I forget that and then the focus goes inward and I fret, and become anxious and concerned with what is happening around me rather than just going down the road.

Galatians 5:22

But when the Holy Spirit controls our lives, he will produce this kind of fruit in us... **one being joy!**

I Didn't Sign Up for a Trip Without Stops!

Difficult circumstances along the way help us to better understand what Christ suffered for us. We get a deeper appreciation of what it cost our Lord as he traveled on this earth. His path led to the cross. I cannot imagine how deeply hurt he was by the fact that when he needed the disciples to be with him... they could not handle it, they were already grieving the loss of what might be happening to their Lord and Savior. They could not even pray with him in the hour of his deepest need. They deserted Him one by one...we might think in our own minds, I would never do that, I would not leave or forsake Him. I would just keep going. I don't always have the discipline required to pray for one hour. I need stops, I need time out...I need to rest. I know myself well enough to tell you my mind wanders and I start thinking about things that are not on the subject. I have to ask the Holy Spirit to discipline my mind. My only hope for making the journey is to renew my mind and focus upon Him.

I also remind myself...the journey is not about me...the destination is not about me. Most of the time, I feel like I am along for the ride...and He is the driver and I am the passenger. I do think sometimes I am the driver, but for the most part, I am a passenger. Happy for the privilege to be in the car.

I've had times when I have been driving down the road and it starts to get boring. I sense myself starting to fall asleep – which is not a good thing. Life can be dull even while we are in the midst of living. We are in the car driving and we need to stay alert. This happens when I lose sight of my destination and what the purpose is for my journey. I am learning to believe that, "As Long As I Am In The Car, I am Not Lost!" I cannot express to you how safe it feels. I am loved with His everlasting love and the journey is what is happening now...but my sights have to be on the final destination. I want my time here to be successful. I want to have meaning and purpose in my life...but I have to rest, and allow Him to take me where he wants and when he wants. I cannot tell the Father how to run his travel agency...or control the strategy of the journey. What a concept for our old nature to think about!

1 Thessalonians 4:15-18

I can tell you this directly from the Lord: We who are still living when the Lord returns will not rise to meet him ahead of those who are in their graves. For the Lord himself will come down from heaven with a commanding shout, with the call of the archangel, and with the trumpet call of God. First, all the Christians who have died will rise from their graves. Then, together with them, we who are still alive and remain on the earth will be caught up in the clouds to meet the Lord in the air and remain with him forever. So comfort and encourage each other with these words.

The journey is important...but unless you know Him...you have no assurance of the destination. I pray that you will invite Christ into your life. He is the one who loves you and gave His life for your sins and mine. I pray we might be ready when the time comes to be caught up in the clouds to meet the Lord in the air and forever be with Him and our loved ones who have joined Him from the graves.

A sobering set of verses from **James 4:7-10**

So humble yourselves before God. Resist the Devil, and he will flee from you. Draw close to God, and God will draw close to you. Wash your hands, you sinners; purify your hearts, you hypocrites. Let there be tears for the wrong things you have done. Let there be sorrow and deep grief. Let there be sadness instead of laughter, and gloom instead of joy. When you bow down before the Lord and admit your dependence on him, he will lift you up and give you honor.

So laughter cannot cover sin...we can not laugh and pretend nothing is happening in our lives, we cannot continue to be the clown if we need to deal with the reality of the journey. We need to seek help and guidance and repent from our wayward ways.

WORTHY EVENTS TO REMEMBER ALONG THE WAY...

1. What is keeping you from stopping along the way and enjoying some down time with the Lord?

2. When was the last time you laughed out loud? What is happening in your life that is robbing you of the joy of the Lord?

3. Does the journey seem tedious to you and boring...what are you going to do to put the joy back into your journey? When will you do that? Maybe you need to ask someone else to drive?

4. Are you prepared for the final lap of the trip? Have you settled the sin question in your life by giving your heart and life to Christ? Wouldn't you like to do that right now?

Pray this prayer...right now.

Lord, I know that I am a sinner. I need to be in the car. I have been wandering around and on many roads, none of which lead to you. Please forgive me, and accept me into your Kingdom. I thank you for dying on the cross for my sins, and even though you were buried, you were raised from the dead, and you are coming back again. I want to be ready to meet you in the air. I do not understand all of this, but I believe it to be true.

Thank you for saving my soul from eternal damnation... which would be hell and out of your presence forever. Thank you for loving me all of this time. Amen.

Chapter Ten ▪━━━

WE'RE ON THE ROAD...

WITHOUT A U-HAUL!

I don't do well with moving and especially the part of following a U-Haul for miles down the road...It is not comforting, knowing all you own is in that small truck going down the road. We may be going to new places and new experiences and hopefully a great and good adventure but the ride behind the U-Haul is not exactly what we expected.

Our world can seem rather small if we view our lives by what is contained in the U-Haul. Our lives cannot be based upon our stuff...what we own, what we are hauling around with us...our lives must have more meaning than stuff...and junk, books...and old furniture!

The U-Haul. → → → → → → → → → → → → → →

The U-Haul is for transporting our goods from one destination to another. When we reach our destination we will not need the U-Haul. When we apply this to our spiritual lives it is a different kind of word picture. We also have no need of what is in the U-Haul when we get to our final destination. Everything we need for today is provided and everything we will need for eternity has been provided.

John 14:2

...I am going to prepare a place for you!

Can you imagine what heaven will be like with the master carpenter preparing it for us? I am sure the cabinets will be at the right level for me or else I will be six feet tall. Either way, I win.

We spend so much time here on this earth, just hauling things around from place to place. We do get attached to our worldly possessions but we cannot take them with us as the old saying goes. It is important in our thinking and in our everyday living, not to attach ourselves to things or people. This is not our final resting place. We cannot take it with us.

Matthew 6:21

Wherever your treasure is, there your heart and thoughts will also be.

When I finally reached the court where my new home was located, I was so thankful. I had followed Tim and the U-Haul...for 800 miles. It was a long tiring trip. I cannot tell you what a relief it was to finally be moved to my new home...close to my family. I had to find a new Church, new friends and in a sense, a new life. I was starting over again. I would be living in a new place without my dear husband Bill. Lots of adjustments ahead for me.

Getting lost for the next few months seemed to almost be normal. It was difficult and I wished I could still be in the car following the U-Haul. It had

given me a sense of knowing where I was in the middle of this long journey...It was a false concept. I needed to shift gears and live each day knowing the Lord was with me. Even when I am feeling alone and lost. I'm really not.

Mom is right...we aren't lost as long as we are in the car...

Sometimes we lose our car on the parking lot and so we now check the alphabetical letters to make sure we can find our car when we come out of the Walmart Store. We're getting smarter in our old age or we have just developed better coping skills.

Possessions and Positions.

We sometimes get caught up with comparing ourselves with others. **Our possessions and the positions we hold.** We compare ourselves with someone we might know in our circle of friends. I can tell you for certain, you do not want what is in my U-Haul...I barely can handle the things I have carried around for years myself. You know it is bad when you can't remember where you got it and what it is for.

I have pictures of people in boxes and albums, if my life depended on it...I couldn't tell you who they are...this sounds like a terrible disease, but in looking at some of my own pictures, the skinny days I call them...it is a little hard to remember those times as well. Life is fleeting and very short. Here today and gone tomorrow.

We are so impressed with our possessions and positions at times we forget to remember we need to be like Paul... Remember his words:

Philippians 3:7-11

I once thought all these things were so very important, but now I consider them worthless because of what Christ has done. Yes, everything else is worthless when compared with the priceless gain of knowing Christ Jesus my Lord. I have discarded everything else, counting it all as garbage, so that I may have

127

Christ and become one with him. I no longer count on my own goodness or my ability to obey God's law, but I trust Christ to save me. For God's way of making us right with himself depends on faith. As a result, I can really know Christ and experience the mighty power that raised him from the dead. I can learn what it means to suffer with him, sharing in his death, so that, somehow, I can experience the resurrection from the dead!

He had it all...and he knew a great deal. He was a very influential man and was respected by many leaders of his time. He was someone to be counted in the hall of fame...but he did not consider any of his possessions or his position to have any validity when it came to the importance of knowing who he was in Christ. When we are faced with the prospects of eternity without Christ...the U-Haul and all of its trappings must be left behind. They become garbage.

The concept of, "Keeping it Simple" and downsizing is truly a freeing gift. I remember a time when Bill was a keeper of important things. He was a pack rat from the word go...several of my sons have carried on this family tradition...but once again, a modern day parable to illustrate this truth.

We lived in this little town in Illinois...and Bill was the Pastor of the First Baptist Church. Times were hard and he was finishing school and doing this little pastorate. We were rich in many ways, but hard pressed for cash. We had a Sale Barn outside of this little town. They gathered on Friday evenings...people took their treasures and had them auctioned off...you could take anything there and the auctioneer would sell it. Bill desperately needed a good white shirt. His shirts were wearing thin on the collars and the cuffs. Mom had turned some of them...but he was needing a white shirt and his birthday was coming...so I wanted to buy him a new shirt.

I went out into the garage and gathered up two bushel baskets of stuff...Bill's stuff and "Sleep", our friend took it to the Sale Barn. It brought a nice sum...and added to what I had been able to save from the grocery money...I bought him a beautiful white shirt. I think he even preached better in that new white shirt...or so it seemed.

Two years later...Bill missed his ball of string...and he was asking, "had I seen it anywhere?" I confessed! He was really upset and said he had been saving that string for almost 5 years. How could I have done such a terrible thing...it had great value to him. He had become attached to his possessions and it didn't matter that he needed a white shirt.

It is much easier to sell another person's treasured stuff than to sell your own. I have also observed this tidbit along the way. We laughed about the missing ball of string for years. When he couldn't find something that seemed lost in our house, he would say, "Is there a Sale Barn near by...your Mom has probably sold it for a good price!"

What things have you become attached to along the way? It may be dragging along behind you as you are traveling around on your path. It could be something very valuable to you, but if it keeps you from being focused on the important things, then it is not good. The weights are hanging on your legs and they are keeping you from running your best race. It is hard to turn the car around with a U-Haul behind you. You have to take a lot into consideration if you are pulling a U-Haul. You can't just stop anywhere along the way, you have to consider what you are pulling along with you and then proceed with caution and care.

Your actions and deeds of kindness and goodness get bogged down by the things you are dragging around with you. You cannot be spontaneous if you are needed in a pinch. You cannot move swiftly to the aid of others if you are worn out by moving your junk around from room to room...or putting it in the car...or packing it into the U-Haul! The cares of this world have taken root and you are not free to serve and minister as you would like.

Carry-On Only. → → → → → → → → → → → → →

I have done a lot of traveling in the car...but I also travel a lot by air. Tim works for one of the larger airlines and I travel to and from conferences and just about any where else I need to go as well. It is a great way to travel...at times I even fly first class which is a real treat. I am not sad when I need to travel first class in order to make my flight...but you can only take a **carry-on piece of luggage.**

You can't carry too much in one piece of small luggage. I have learned to mix and match, to pack things that will not wrinkle... and I must think in terms of weather, hoping I have chosen to bring the right kind of clothes to suit the weather...but it takes some planning and thinking and you simply can't take all those shoes.

As Christians and world travelers...we think we should be able to take it all with us. We want all of the comforts of home to be at our disposal. I would like to bring that big bulky robe I enjoy wearing just before I go to bed...but it is not possible. It is too much to cram into my little carry-on bag.

In the Christian life...we are challenged to be careful what we bring along for the journey. I know some of us carry things into our marriages from our past that are bulky and cumbersome. We have become accustomed to unhealthy behaviors and we bring those behaviors into our marriages and families...we talked about this topic in chapter one...God says for us to let the past be past – Leave and cling!

> **Philippians 3:13-14**
> *No dear friends, I am still not all I should be, but I am focusing all my energies on this one thing: Forgetting the past and looking forward to what lies ahead, I strain to reach the end of the race and receive the prize for which God, through Christ Jesus, is calling us up to heaven.*

Philippians 3:20

But we are citizens of heaven, where the Lord Jesus Christ lives. And we are eagerly waiting for Him to return as our Savior. He will take these weak mortal bodies of ours and change them into glorious bodies like his own, using the same mighty power that he will use to conquer everything, everywhere.

The U-Haul and the Carry-On...when I consider what I can carry it isn't very much. When I can use a U-Haul it is quite a lot. I think about downsizing and not taking on a lot of responsibility by gathering things unto myself...but it is not an easy task. The concept is in my head but the actuality of living it out is quite another story. Making the application to my lifestyle is where the rubber meets the road.

Why are People Living in Their Cars? → → → → → →

When I think of people who are living in their cars...it makes me sad. I feel so blessed to have all I have. We could say, they deserve it because of poor management, or we could judge them based upon thinking more of ourselves than we should... but the Lord has really convicted me concerning the selfishness of man. I have a house where I live alone. True, I share my home with others from time to time who are in need of shelter. I could do more but for now, that is what I can do and the Lord blesses my life over and over again.

People would not have to live in cars and streets if it were not for the selfishness of man. I think about how people feed pets while people are starving. I realize this is a very harsh statement to those who might have pets...but we have enough money and food in this world for everyone to have something to eat every day. Our selfishness is not something any of us can be proud of...we joke about sending the used tea bags to the missionaries...but we all know it is the selfishness of man that gets in the way of sharing and being truly equal. Jesus reminded us, "We would have the poor with us always," ...and that is because of our selfishness. It is also an opportunity to give rather than receive. If we are to be givers... then someone has to be able to receive.

Selfishness goes way back. Remember Lot and Abraham...and Lot took a long look at the fertile plains...and Lot chose that land for himself. **Genesis 13:8-13**

Remember Jacob and his father in-law...Jacob was forced to work for seven years for Rachel only to have his father in-law give him the wrong daughter...so he ended up working another seven years. What was that all about anyway? Could it be selfishness? **Genesis 29:14-30**

Genesis 28:20-22

*Then Jacob made this vow: "If God will be with me and protect me on this **journey** and give me food and clothing, and if he will bring me back safely to my father, then I will make the LORD my God. This memorial pillar it will become a place for worshiping God, and I will give God a tenth of everything He gives me."*

Selfishness keeps us from honoring God and others. Remember the couple in the New Testament.

Acts 5:1-11

There was also a man named Ananias who, with his wife, Sapphira, sold some property. He brought part of the money to the apostles, but he claimed it was the full amount. His wife had agreed to this deception.

Then Peter said, "Ananias, why has Satan filled your heart? You lied to the Holy Spirit, and you kept some of the money for yourself. The property was yours to sell or not sell, as you wished. And after selling it, the money was yours to give away. How could you do a thing like this? You weren't lying to us but to God."

As soon as Ananias heard these words, he fell to the floor and died. Everyone who heard about it was terrified. Then some young men wrapped him in a sheet and took him out and buried him.

About three hours later his wife came in, not know-ing what had happened. Peter asked her, "Was this the price you and your husband received for your land?" "Yes," she replied, "that was the price."

And Peter said, "How could the two of you even think of doing a thing like this—conspiring together to test the Spirit of the Lord? Just outside that door are the young men who buried your husband, and they will carry you out, too."

Instantly, she fell to the floor and died. When the young men came in and saw that she was dead, they carried her out and buried her beside her husband. Great fear gripped the entire church and all others who heard what had happened.

What are we carrying around...what are we dragging behind us? Selfishness destroys relationships and families.

Philippians 2:4

Don't think only about your own affairs, but be interested in others, too, and what they are doing.

We **are** our brother's keepers. Selfishness keeps us from learning about the needs of others and we end up putting ourselves first.

My granddaughters had a time of fasting and doing projects to help others. It was a Youth Group Event to help them think about and remember oth-ers who are less fortunate. They are young and they are learning from their church and from their family about denying themselves and putting others first...It is not some-thing we should take lightly. We need to learn to sacrifice and share what we have with others. We cannot model this or do this too early. They need to grasp the concept of help-ing and serving others. Families need to think about these things and we need to give opportunities for those in our church body to live out their faith in practical ways.

It's a dog-eat-dog world unless we determine with God's help to make a difference. We cannot expect the government to take care of the poor and to make the lives of others better. It is the responsibility and calling of the Church. We have neglected this area of the journey for such a long time. I remember my Mom modeling this truth for me in a special way:

> *We would often go to the resale shop and Mom would pick up cups and saucers at a very cheap price, even old dishes. It was not for us...but for the "bums" that would come to our door. I was not allowed to call these people "bums"...but I did behind her back. I know by today's standards and terms, they would be called "street people". They would come around to our back door and ask for a dime. Mom would not give them money, because she supposed they would use the money to buy a drink. She would prepare them a cup of coffee with a saucer...and make them a sandwich with whatever she might have and give them a napkin and perhaps a cookie or two...or even a piece of pie...they would sit on our back porch and have a "little lunch," as Mom referred to it.*

I realize they marked the curb...and they knew they could stop at our house for a "little lunch" anytime. This is a good memory I have of my Mother's kindness. We didn't have very much ourselves, but we shared with those less fortunate.

Matthew 16:23

Jesus turned to Peter and said, "Get away from me, Satan! You are a dangerous trap to me. You are seeing things merely from a human point of view, and not from God's."

The more you think of yourself, the harder it is to find eternal life.

We often think if we cannot do something huge, we won't do

anything. We need to be faithful in the small things...knowing God will bless it. The boy only had 2 fishes and 5 barley loaves...and God increased it. He multiplies our efforts and He blesses us...based upon His faithfulness to His people and to His word. I love being part of building the Kingdom and doing Kingdom work.

Ecclesiastes 11:4-6

If you wait for perfect conditions, you will never get anything done.

God's ways are as hard to discern as the pathways of the wind, and as mysterious as a tiny baby being formed in a mother's womb.

Be sure to stay busy and plant a variety of crops, for you never know which will grow—perhaps they all will.

We're on the Road...and we aren't lost. We have places to go and things to do. We are taking advantage of the modern day methods of transportation. We are E-mailing while our world becomes smaller and smaller. We can view today's events around the world even as they are happening. We are global in every sense of the word...except in how we are living out our faith. We often think in terms of me and mine...and we need to think in terms of our world...our sisters and brothers in different parts of the world. How can we help? How can we practice loving others when we are so focused on our own needs. I do think we need to love ourselves as we love others, but often the love process gets broken down...and we are sitting at the edge of the road...waiting for someone to help us... when we could be extending help to those along our path.

Psalm 25:4

Show me the path where I should walk, O LORD; point out the right road for me to follow.

Ecclesiastes 10:14

Foolish people claim to know all about the future and tell everyone the details! But who can really know what is going to happen?

135

The Lord is coming soon...and he will thankfully rescue us from the cares and concerns of this world. We will have finally arrived...my bag isn't packed...but I can tell you...I am ready!

I want my life to count. I want the trip to have meaning and purpose. I want to be able to look back at the journey with a sense of God's presence in my life. I want to make a difference.

Romans 15:2

We should please others. If we do what helps them, we will build them up in the Lord.

I'm in the Car...and I'm not lost.

WORTHY EVENTS TO REMEMBER ALONG THE WAY...

We have lots to consider as we close out this chapter...first concern I have, is to be sure you know who you are in Christ? Are you in the Car? I trust you have considered the importance of knowing Him...the journey is impossible without His guidance in our lives.

1. Has your U-Haul become impossible to park? Maybe you need to find a place for some of the junk and give it away. Give your anxieties and concerns to the one who cares for you.

2. Carry-On...trying to pack more into your life than really needs to be there? What action do you need to take...to stop the craziness in your life?

3. Selfishness is a topic no one wants to discuss...but how can we do a reality check of how we are living out our faith without discussing selfishness. Possessions and Positions are not important without the Lord being the Lord of it all.

Selfishness is the divisive force threatening every relationship we have. The weakness of allowing the pursuit of getting our needs met as well as the destructive obsessions we take unto ourselves is the dark force behind all sin. It is not anger, pride, hatred, or malice...although it can be found in all of these. It is the simple everyday garden variety sin called selfishness. From Adam and Eve...and the forbidden fruit to our present world. The seductive power of selfishness leads many off into streets and roads that are not heading in the right direction where they want to go.

Proverbs 14:2

Those who follow the right path fear the LORD; those who take the wrong path despise Him.

Proverbs 14:8

The wise look ahead to see what is coming, but fools deceive themselves.

Proverbs 14:12

There is a path before each person that seems right, but it ends in death.

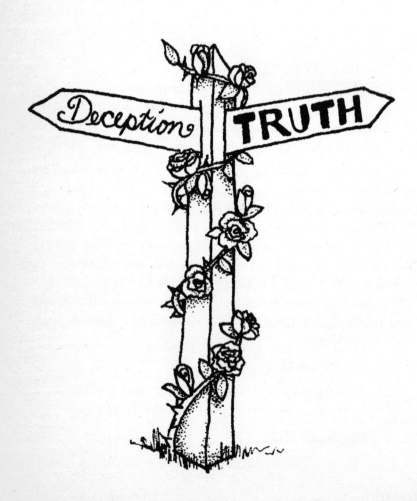

NOTES

NOTES

NOTES

NOTES